ENDORSEMENTS FOR CRYSTAL LOVE

"For such a time as this, Crystal Love releases her memoir in a new book entitled *Finding Normal*. Each chapter is a melody that will delight and inspire the reader to experience love, embrace healing, and discover God's purpose. Now is the time to purchase a book that will change your life."

— APOSTLE LINDA HARVEY, AUTHOR OF DEVOTIONS FOR EVERYDAY WOMEN OF FAITH

"In the midst of abnormal, challenging times, people are looking for answers. In the book, *Finding Normal*, Crystal Love challenges us all to look at ourselves. She confronts us with what we need to do and gives us solid, practical help in reminding us of what we are called to be. Even mature believers can glean from her vivid illustrations, which are common to all of us. After all, the stakes are very high! Our calling, our destiny, and our future are worth our peace."

— DR. G, CLINICAL CHRISTIAN COUNSELOR

"*Finding Normal* is an amazing journey of discovery. Crystal Love shares how her trust in God to guide her mind, body, and spirit allowed her to discover her God-given purpose. She reminds her readers that normal is really between you and God. Trusting Him, while keeping your ear to His mouth, is the only way to discover and walk in your normalcy. Crystal's delivery shows her ability to be vulnerable, as the readers get a chance to see deep into her soul. At each level, from acknowledging God's presence to letting Him take over and reshape your life, Crystal shows us step-by-step how to move closer and closer to God. As an educator, this book is an example of exemplary writing. As a Christian, it is a true blessing and the key to finding your unique relationship with God.

Finding Normal reminds us that there's nothing in this world that two people can't do, as long as one is God, and the other is you!"

— JANICE F. WILLIAMS, RETIRED HIGH SCHOOL PRINCIPAL BALTIMORE CITY PUBLIC SCHOOLS

"Crystal Love is a passionate and radical lover of Christ, who captures the heart of the reader. Crystal is a business owner, mother, wife, and friend to many. One thing that Crystal can share with the world through this book is how to be content in all circumstances. Contentment is a great gain and brings us much peace. That alone is a huge gift to share with so many. Her testimony and revelation will bring victory to others. Authenticity and healing are dominant throughout this book. There is such a passion for embracing all circumstances in our life— after all— this is the heart of the Father.

Throughout this book, you will find healing for yourself. Destiny doesn't come without cost. The pain intertwined with the joys of life can bring about an awestruck beauty to existence. You will develop true freedom through reading this. The author is boldly authentic and carries this over into the spirit of the book. I love true authors that write from their own experience and not just knowledge. As a reader, you can get a sense and know the difference. This will make others look at their life and say it is okay not to be normal— after all, what is normal? In Chapter 7, you will see how God created you to be an extraordinary design. This is a book you must read! It will change your life forever.

When you read *Finding Normal*, your victory will help someone else. Someone else's victory is attached to your testimony. You have meaning, and through *Finding Normal*, it will begin your next steps to freedom, love, boldness, healing, peace, and destiny. It sounds simple, but so many of us need to walk in these gifts. This book will develop you in a way that you will become balanced in all things. It will bless you in this season. Crystal has a pure heart and sets the truth before you. She shares her soul to help you overcome all things through the greatest depth of love. This will be passed on to you as you read *Finding Normal*. Enjoy your time with this book. And with great love and joy sent to you, we wish you blessings and freedom!"

— DAVID AND TRACY WHITTINGTON, PASTORS OF
REDEMPTION HOUSE LIFE CENTER

FINDING NORMAL

Crystal Love

Edited by Nicole Queen

Copyright © 2021 Crystal Love

All rights reserved.

This book is established to provide information and inspiration to all readers. It is designed with the understanding that the author is not engaged to render any psychological, legal, or any other kind of professional advice. The content is the sole expression of the author. All events, locales, and conversations have been recreated based on the author's memory. And to maintain anonymity, some names have purposely been excluded. In addition, some identifying details have been left out to protect the privacy of specific individuals and the integrity of the author's experiences with them. The author is not liable for any physical, psychological, emotional, financial, or commercial damages, including, but not limited to special, incidental, consequential, or other damages. All readers are responsible for their own choices, actions, and results.

No part of this book may be reproduced in any form or by electronic or mechanical means, including information storage and retrieval systems, without written permission from the author, except for the use of brief quotations in a book review.

ISBN: 978-1-955297-92-9 (Hardback)
LCCN: 2021915610

Title Your Truth Publishing
9103 Woodmore Centre #334
Lanham, MD 20706

www.titleyourtruthpublishing.com

In loving memory of Jacob and Exemea Schroeder, you left an imprint of grace on my heart. Your sacrifice will never be forgotten.

"I can do all things through Christ who strengthens me."

— PHILIPPIANS 4:3

CONTENTS

Foreword	xv
Preface	xvii
Introduction	xxv
1. EMBRACE YOUR BREAKING POINTS	1
My Childhood Years	1
My Preadolescent Years	7
My Teenage Years	15
My Adulthood Years	20
2. PICK UP THE PIECES	37
3. BE HEALED	47
David & The Amalekites	48
Heal The Wound	49
4. MIND WHAT MATTERS	57
In The Beginning	57
My Pregnancy with Joshua	59
Consider the Seeds You Sow	60
Take Responsibility	62
5. FOCUS FOR PRODUCTIVITY	69
What Can You See?	69
Get Back On Course	70
6. BE SHOCKED	79
Welcome to North Carolina	79
Do You Fit?	81
Living Spiritually in the Flesh	83
Culture Shock	84
It's Time For Change	84
Trust & Obey	86

7. BEND TO BLEND	99
Don't Compromise to Fit In	100
You Are Enough	101
8. SET YOUR THERMOMETER	107
Welcome to Hair Chemistry	108
Where Is Your Setting?	109
Get Uncomfortable	109
9. WALK IN MINISTRY	117
Discovering My Purpose	118
Life Before Christ	120
Addictions	122
New Life With Christ	127
Fulfill Your Purpose	128
Know When It's Time To Move Forward	130
My Spiritual Development	131
My Spiritual Blessings	132
10. KEEP MOVING	139
Address The Root	139
Keep Growing	141
11. BE CONFIDENT ABOUT YOUR VISION	147
Discover Vision Early	148
Speak Life	148
Make Your Plan	149
Move Forward	150
Appreciate You	150
Be Bold & Believe	151
Have Vision	152
Examples of Visionaries	152
Launch Your Vision	154
12. PASS THE BATON	161
A Testimony of Grace	162
After You've Cried A River	169
13. HAVE FAITH IN YOUR FUTURE	179
If Only…	179
Maintain Your Posture Of Faith	180
Intrinsic Faith	181

14. ACCEPT YOUR NORMAL	187
Your First Choice	189
This Is How It's Supposed To Be	189
Transition & Birth	192
Purpose Revealed	194
Jesus Is The Example	195
Receive By Faith	196
Commune Through Your Senses	198
Be Authentic	207
The Inside War	208
Stay Connected	209
Get Cleaned	210
New Life By The Blood of Jesus	211
15. FINISH STRONG	219
Finishing High School	219
Finishing College & Vocational Certifications	221
Finishing My Life Story	222
Finish Your Story	224
Afterword	227
Acknowledgments	231
About the Author	239

FOREWORD

Hello, Beloveds!

My name is Darlene Curry. I'm a radical lover of God, wife, mother, and creative. Crystal Love is one of my beloved spiritual daughters, adopted by heart, and is a sheer delight to my heart. If I could use one word to describe her, the word I would choose is *tenacious*.

---

te·na·cious /təˈnāSHəs/ *adjective*
- tending to keep a firm hold of something; clinging or adhering closely
- preserving, persistent, determined, pertinacious, resolute and steadfast

---

Crystal Love has a passion for becoming everything that the Creator had in mind for her to become, as He knit her together in her mother's womb. But her passion goes far beyond that. She deeply desires to co-labor with God to empower others to find their normal, even in the midst of chaos, through the lens of truth.

FOREWORD

Indeed, what is normal anyway?

---

nor·mal /ˈnôrməl/ *adjective*
- conforming to a standard; usual, typical, or expected

Romans 12:2 tells us to:

> "Stop imitating the ideals and opinions of the culture around [us], but [to] be inwardly transformed by the Holy Spirit through a total reformation of how [we] think. This will empower [us] to discern God's will, as [we] live a beautiful life, satisfying and perfect in His eyes."

As you journey through *Finding Normal*, it will greatly aid in the metamorphosis of your life. You'll find raw transparency and truth. Crystal holds nothing back, but fully gives herself to the hand of her Maker. False mindsets will fall off, and you'll be deeply encouraged, as you begin to discern and see yourself through the heart and mind of God. Crystal has given and continues to give herself to the process of total transformation that leads to freedom! This freedom can be yours, too, if you choose a life of surrender to the One who knows you best!

Darlene Curry, Co-Pastor
Seek His Face Ministries

PREFACE

Many days I prayed: "I just want to be normal," but didn't understand the magnitude of what I wanted. *What drove me to say this? And where did that thought come from? Did I really want to have a typical life?* The simple answer to this question was *no*. But in hindsight, that answer was a bit more complicated. What I truly desired was the life that God predestined and planned for me. That was my normal. But at the time, I didn't know it. God had a plan for my pain.

In life, there may be times when it feels like the pain of our suffering is unique to others. Intense pain may distort our understanding of reality and leave us feeling as if no one else is privy to our experiences. We may think that our life is shattered and far from normal, thinking that no one can relate. But the truth is, normal isn't the same for everyone. My normal is *my* normal; your normal is *yours*! And perhaps this book is the answer you've been searching for.

Normalcy— is that what we really want? Like myself, many have wondered what normal life was like and if it could ever be attained. In pursuit of these answers, this book uncovers profound truths surrounding the notion of living what appears to be normal, alongside strategic glimpses

PREFACE

into my past and current reality. Culturally, we tend to live life from the perspective of what we perceive as normal or socially acceptable. *But what exactly is normal? Is it the same for everyone?*

The truth is, we may never know how our normal compares to another's normal. My normal may be vastly different or intriguingly similar to yours. If given a chance to trade places with us, there may be someone who would gladly welcome the opportunity to do so. For whatever reason, our normal may not be what we desire, but conversely, it may be the highlight of someone else's life. At times, we may not appreciate our normalcy due to its lack of change. Our normal routine may cause us to feel stagnant and bored, which may be the epitome of frustration for some. Although it is more likely for those who live within a dysfunctional environment to crave normalcy, many who are well-off may even have a desire for their lives to be normal. For the person accustomed to suffering, the normalcy craved could be the absence of pain. For the wealthy person, the normalcy craved could be the desire for privacy and simple living. Therefore, it's worthy to note that normalcy means different things to different people. And oftentimes, it's not until the desire is expressed that change begins to take place.

When we can accept our current reality and make a conscious decision to produce another outcome, we have opened the door for change. *Is change a viable possibility? Do we have the ability to produce it?* Absolutely! Most times, change doesn't require physical adjustments. Oftentimes, it's our perspective that needs to be adjusted. We cannot allow our posture to be negatively impacted by what we see. We must maintain an open heart that is teachable, willing to learn, and able to adjust.

Simply stated, we must accept the reality of our own truth. Although my challenge may be simple for you to navigate, as yours may be effortless for me, we are ultimately responsible for our own. We must come to terms with facing our own reality. Sometimes, that may mean admitting that we need help. Our humility before God is often the first step towards experiencing the lasting change we desire to see.

PREFACE

"I know what it means to lack, and I know what it means to experience overwhelming abundance. For I'm trained in the secret of overcoming all things, whether in fullness or hunger. And I find that the strength of Christ's explosive power infuses me to conquer every difficulty."

— PHILIPPIANS 4:12-13

Regardless of circumstance, God's strength is made perfect in our weakness. Knowing this creates a satisfying resolve. Our *normal* can never supersede the power of His strength. But sometimes, it takes the experience of your own journey to understand this truth. Through glimpses into my past, this book captures my journey throughout the discovery, appreciation, and acceptance of *my* normalcy, with attempts of helping you to recognize and receive yours. I pray that your journey reveals the strength of God's power and the beauty of *your* normal.

SPECIAL RESOURCES

30 Day Devotional

Please note that are many references to the 30 Day Devotional throughout this special edition book. The 30 Day Devotional will be available for purchase in November 2021.

Strategies of Finding Normal

Please access the website or scan below to access the free masterclass and e-book.

Website: www.crystallove-theauthor.com/special-edition-finding-normal-video-clips/

Please note that all scans are direct links to specific items. All items can be found on the main website.

Website: www.crystallove-theauthor.com

RESOURCES FOR THE INTRODUCTION

Purchase your "I Am" affirmation t-shirt today by scanning below.

Purchase your "Finding Normal Be Uniquely You" t-shirt today by scanning below.

Answer the following questions before you get started...

What have you imagined you'd already become?
1.
2.
3.

What three goals will help you achieve this?
1.
2.
3.

RESOURCES FOR THE INTRODUCTION

If you would like virtual or in-person Vision Advance sessions, scan below to schedule your free your consultation.

Scan below to hear affirmation audios. For access, use the password: Listen.

INTRODUCTION

What is normal? When you really think about it, its true implications may surprise you. Aside from popular belief, *normal* doesn't necessitate easiness or the absence of pain. Normal living isn't synonymous with simple living. However, its true definition reveals that it's the nature of conforming to a standard or being typical. So, why do we liken the idea of normalcy to a fantasy world where everything is peachy-keen? The problem, therefore, lies in our perspective. And our perspective is often shaped by our influences and what we see.

It wasn't uncommon for me to frequent the idea of life outside of my worldview. I often observed other families, while imagining how life would be if I were in their shoes. Although I genuinely appreciated my family and the vast opportunities I was given, I sometimes wondered how different my life could've been.

As the daughter of two powerful ministers of the gospel, I grew up in a God-centered home. Growing up in a home that reverenced Christ provided me with a strong foundation in the Word of God. Ministry was our way of life; it was my normal. But as I grew older, I challenged those norms because I viewed many things differently.

As a child, you may grow up indoctrinated in a certain way of life, regardless of your understanding at the time. Some things you just do

INTRODUCTION

because you're instructed to do so— no questions asked! However, as you develop, you may tend to question the very things you followed so closely.

When I reached adulthood, I realized that there were many things that I didn't understand. As time went on, my ignorance faded, and I became more aware of life's truths. One significant truth I discovered was that a relationship with God isn't void of challenging situations. Walking with God provides you with His insight, understanding, and strength, as you tackle difficulties that are essential to your predestined norm.

YOU ARE VICTORIOUS

Although not desired, difficulties are sometimes essential to your norm. I've observed many people endure a lifestyle of challenges, and with the grace of God, successfully overcome them. Watching the way they handled their challenging moments has helped me get through my similarly rough situations. Oftentimes, many don't realize that their journey from struggle to victory can be someone else's saving grace. I've personally been encouraged by the testimony of others who have continued to fight through their tumultuous times. After encountering many challenges, I've realized that overcoming each setback has contributed towards the composite of who I am— the portrait of who God has created me to be. Amidst those circumstances, I discovered His peace.

It may be hard to appreciate God's peace until you've gone through a challenge and experienced His love. His very presence brings change. And because of His compassion, He may choose to adjust the situation or reshape your heart towards it.

YOU ARE COVERED

When our hearts are bitter towards a situation, our inability to see and process clearly may be the consequence of our own obscurity. It may require us to look deeper at the situation to zero in on the controlling factors that may have disrupted our balance. Focused thinking may help us release and process what may be deeply rooted in our minds. Our

INTRODUCTION

subconscious may be overwhelmed with a plethora of unaddressed feelings, questionable thoughts, and painful memories-- waiting patiently to be processed. Although confronting those inner thoughts may help us understand our choices, our busyness is often accepted as a convenient scapegoat.

Our non-compliance to prioritize the time for our wellbeing is why we desperately need God to balance everything out. As with all issues of life, His divine assistance is essential to confronting matters that we may otherwise choose to conceal or not know how to handle.

"Call to me, and I will answer you and tell you great and unsearchable things you do not know."

— JEREMIAH 33:3

The truth is, only He knows what true freedom and balance are for us. Apart from Him, we cannot attain the stability that we need to continue moving forward.

YOU ARE DESTINED

To maintain stability, it's essential to recognize the presence of distractions that may surface. A distraction can be anything that forcibly grabs our attention and robs us of our focus. Therefore, we must be determined not to allow extreme or minor distractions to take us off of our preordained paths— not even for a second. Some distractions have the potential to prevent us from giving our attention to things of value. They may cause us to become agitated and lose focus. Such agitations may be brief or seemingly endless, but regardless, it's our responsibility to appropriately address them upon their arrival.

A choice must be made. Are you going to allow a distraction to stop you or slow you down? Or, are you going to turn what was meant to derail you into a launching pad to build your momentum? It's *your* deci-

INTRODUCTION

sion! In moments of distress, we can choose to nurture our frustrations and give power to the distraction or choose to move forward. What will *you* decide? No one can make this choice for us, not even God. Even He gives us free will. We must be bold enough to make the right decision, and with God's divine help, move forward— no matter how difficult it may be.

YOU ARE CAPABLE

You may be asking: *Why do things have to be so complicated?* Complexity is a matter of perspective. But instead of focusing on things outside of our control, our efforts should be spent preparing to handle whatever comes our way. We may not know the answer to the *why*, but we do know The *Who*.

"Trust in the LORD with all thine heart and lean not unto thine own understanding. In all thy ways acknowledge Him, and He shall direct thy paths."

— PROVERBS 3:5-6

God desires for us to put our confidence in Him when times are good, and when times are bad. Our efforts do not compare to His sovereignty. His all-powerful and all-knowing nature can help us through the most challenging times.

When times get rough, we may be inclined to look at another person's life and wonder: "Can I just have *that* normal life?" Most times, we may desire to switch places with someone in moments of discouragement, wishing things were different. But let's take a moment to think about what we're really asking. *Do we really want another person's norms?* And what about the parts of their lives that we don't always see? Feeling disheartened, we may contemplate: "If only I looked different, had different parents, and was brought up in a different environment

INTRODUCTION

— *that* life would've been better!" We may even wonder what life would be like with more money or the opportunity to go back in time and make better decisions! *If only, if only!* The truth is, decisions are made every day. And sometimes we don't understand the consequences of our actions until later.

YOU ARE FORGIVEN

The decisions we make are oftentimes based upon our current mindset and understanding. So we must not be overwhelmed with the *what-ifs* of life; we must be able to accept what is and move on from that place. And over time, we can make wiser decisions as we mature in our understanding.

Throughout this process, we must not live in regret. We must understand that despite our mistakes, God has given us unmerited grace to accomplish His purpose for our lives. We must be willing to forgive ourselves, as those decisions may have been made before understanding our purpose in life.

YOU ARE PURPOSED

So now, we must be honest with ourselves. *Do we really know our purpose—the reason for our existence?* Perhaps you've pondered these questions, as well: *Who am I? Does my life have meaning? Am I here to do something?* The answers to those questions are crucial towards making wise decisions, as everything we do should reflect our God-ordained purpose.

Every action we take should be purpose-driven. Each step should be towards fulfilling our purpose, no matter how small it may be. Every effort matters, as fulfilling purpose takes time, discipline, and determination.

Imagine if God called you to be a missionary. Your purpose may be to travel internationally to spread the Gospel of Jesus. *But how would you begin? Would you quit your current job and jump on the next flight to Japan? How would it be possible to fulfill this colossal purpose?* It may seem as if God's purpose for your life is massive and unattainable based on your own

INTRODUCTION

strength and capabilities. The truth is, many people have adopted this perception and don't believe that they have what it takes to accomplish what they were designed to fulfill. For a moment, consider the mouthwatering taste of a rich, moist slice of cake. Before a baker attempts to make a cake, the exact ingredients are known before the cooking process begins. Having the right ingredients assures the baker that the cake will be delicious and moist. When the cake is complete, it may initially appeal to others through its visual beauty and captivating smell. Soon afterward, they may want to taste it, to fully experience its goodness. Similarly, your life is an ingredient to the perfect recipe that was designed to be appealing, but ultimately, a mouthwatering blessing for others.

YOU ARE RELATIONAL

In order to know which paths to take in life, you must have a relationship with the One who created you and established your purpose. Having a relationship with God is the key to discovering everything about you and your journey in life. Although He does not tell us everything ahead of time, He effectively communicates what we need at the time. Sometimes, telling us a lot can be too much for us to handle all at once. Oftentimes, He reveals it to us one task at a time— one vision at a time. Even then, what may appear to be a lot of information may only be the tip of the iceberg, as it pertains to His ultimate plan for your life.

When I reflect on the work of God throughout the many seasons of my life, it leaves me in awe. I recall being in a state of despondency, due to having an inaccurate perception of my current season at the time. Eventually, I learned not to judge any season by how I feel at the present moment. I had to accept that I can't depend on my emotions to make life-altering decisions because they aren't always as reliable as God's truth. Our hearts control our will and emotions. It can affect how productive we are in life.

INTRODUCTION

"Create in me a clean heart, O God…"

— PSALMS 51:10

Without a pure heart, we won't be able to think clearly and make rational decisions. Therefore, we must strive to keep our hearts clean, which comes through our relationship with Christ.

Although God desires us to be in relationships, some relationships that we've formed throughout life were not a part of His intention. They may have been developed by chance and opportunity. *So, should we live life with regret?* Absolutely not! We cannot erase the past. What's done is done! But we can consider the type of people we attract.

YOU ARE CONNECTED

Have you ever noticed that you may attract people dealing with the same challenge you've dealt with? Depending on where you are in the process, you may be able to help others dealing with a problem you've overcome. Once you are healed, you may be able to be a mentor to others in search of the healing that you received. We are all spiritual beings that connect to others for many different reasons.

God may send someone to you to meet a need. However, He may impose limits; He doesn't want us to become dependent on others to fulfill a void that only He can satisfy. God desires to be our priority and to be put first in all things. Even when we seek assistance from friends and loved ones, He must be our number one source. God is the only one who can bring us true contentment.

God may connect us to others for the sake of enjoyment, enhancement, or evangelism. Although He may use us as His vessels, we must remember that He performs the work of healing and salvation. He is the true source of every need.

In times of crisis, we may be tempted to reach out to others before reaching out to God. *But what happens if every call you make to your friends and family goes to voicemail? What if everyone you try to reach is unavailable?* God does not want to be our last resort. He should be our first choice — *always*.

Have you ever been in a relationship where neither person could assist the other? What if the relationship was like oil and water? No matter how much you try to make it blend, it never thoroughly mixes! Regardless of it not being the connection you may have desired it to be, it can still serve a higher purpose. God is intentional about everything He ordains. Nothing catches Him by surprise.

Situations in life may catch you off guard. Such moments may have evoked an impulsive reaction that caught you by surprise. *Does that response define who you are?* Absolutely not! As humans, we have the potential to step entirely out of character, if provoked. It may be hard to process afterward, as you may not be able to recognize yourself at that moment. We may have suppressed feelings that were never released or resolved. This can lead to questionable behavior, producing an eruption of emotions that may overhaul your actions, and ultimately, a loss of control.

YOU ARE TRANSFORMED

The Word of God states that there is no good thing in the flesh. Unless we acknowledge our frailty and submit our ways to God, we will continue to surprise ourselves with actions we didn't think we were capable of doing. When we submit ourselves to God, He will begin to change our hearts, as we become more like Him. We will start developing and exemplifying His nine attributes, commonly referred to as The Fruit of the Holy Spirit.

One Fruit of the Spirit is temperance. This attribute is based upon moderation, which reveals the value God places on the principle of demonstrating self-control, self-restraint, and self-discipline. Becoming disciplined isn't easy. It not only requires humility, but a willingness to be sustained through the help of the Holy Spirit. He may send support through the constructive criticism of another who has the heart of God and your best interest at heart. We must be careful not to reject His help, but to be humble when we are out of line. Being corrected may not be

INTRODUCTION

easy, but having the right company can cause us to attract the right people. When we are submitted to God's process, we may begin to attract others who are also following His plan for their lives. This creates a healthy space for us to learn, grow, and be accountable to others when making mistakes.

Mistakes are inevitable. No one is perfect. And we cannot change the past. But, we can take ownership of our mistakes, learn, grow, and pass its lessons on to others.

YOU ARE NORMAL

As the recipient of much wisdom, I am grateful for those who have gone through challenges, overcame them, and regained their lives. My growth is a product of their mistakes and flaws. Through various facets, I received vital information that has shaped my life today. Over time, I accrued a wealth of wisdom through seminars, sermons, and social media sources, just to name a few. Through the transparency and boldness of others, I grew to understand the significance of my journey and what constituted the essence of my normalcy.

But despite the shame and guilt, I endured the process of self-forgiveness and was open to receive God's healing. Being healed allowed me to see that despite my mistakes, all that transpired formed the essence of *my normal*.

RESOURCES FOR CHAPTER ONE

Refer to the 30 Day Devotional
Day 3: "Take The Positive Out Of The Negative"
(*Available November 2021*)

Refer to Strategies of Finding Normal
"Overcoming Abandonment & Forgiveness"

Scan the QR code below to download the strategies.

For Access
Use Password: Listen

Listen to the Declaration of Healing from Abandonment, Prayer of Forgiveness, and Prayer of Healing from Divorce.

For Access
Use Password: Listen

RESOURCES FOR CHAPTER ONE

Many of us have gone through life and encountered many traumatic situations that we didn't know how to deal with. When these situations aren't dealt with properly, it will lead to a life of painful cycles.

Our counseling sessions will help you walk through those difficult times in your life, teach you how to filter your thoughts, and manage them properly.

Our counseling sessions are based upon Biblical principles from the Word of God. We will walk you through healing and deliverance from the various issues you may have faced from childbirth until now. We are here to walk you through this process, however long it takes.

Scan below for your free counseling consultation.

1

EMBRACE YOUR BREAKING POINTS

*I*n life, we may experience various breaking points. Breaking points can occur as a response to copious amounts of pressure or stress. Although each situation may be different, each circumstance helps to define our limitations. Throughout my childhood, preadolescent, teenage, and adulthood years, I experienced various breaking points that not only revealed my threshold for pressure, but enabled me to see the grace of God on my life.

MY CHILDHOOD YEARS

Born and raised in Baltimore, Maryland, I lived in the middle-class community. Some of the streets we lived on included: Gilmore St, Greenmount Ave, Marble Hall Rd, N. Edgecombe Circle, and Church Lane. We primarily stayed in East Baltimore, but later transitioned to West Baltimore.

One day, when we lived on Gilmore St., I wanted to go outside and play with my brothers. It was a snowy day, but I had no snow boots. So, my parents took plastic bags and tied them over my shoes so that I could play with my older brothers Eric and Tony in the snow. Boy, those were the days! Although I had fun, I didn't stay out too long, because after a short while, my feet were cold and the thrill was gone! And because I was a girl, they made sure my feet were warmed first.

The memory of growing up as the only girl had its perks! I always had my own room, while my brothers shared a room with either twin beds or bunk beds. But even though I had my private space, I was always around them, and very seldom stayed in my room alone. But when I did, my time alone consisted of practicing hairstyles on my Barbie dolls. And at an early age, my passion for hair began.

At the end of a long day, our typical bedtime was 8:00, but Thursdays were a treat because we would sit at the end of our parent's bed to watch the Cosby Show that aired at 8:00 pm. We didn't have TVs in our room, so we enjoyed watching television with our parents. Today, very few families spend time together in front of the television or a movie. In today's society, most children have their own television, phone, tablet, and computer. My how times changed! Back then, Thursday nights gave us something to look forward to. And in my little world as a child, I was so happy and content.

My School Life

As a young girl, I woke up around 6:30 am on a typical weekday. However, this was very difficult for me, because little did I know, I wasn't a morning person.

One day, I didn't want to get up for school. So, I tried everything I could do to get out of going to school that morning. That particular morning, I was sleepy, but it wasn't because I stayed up late. So instead of ironing my clothes regularly, I decided to lay across my bed and iron my clothes. Needless to say, that wasn't a good idea, as I burned the inside of my elbow. And to this day, I still have the scar. Let's just say that that was the last time I tried that move.

In general, my normal routine consisted of waking up, taking a shower, getting dressed, and walking to school. Being at school was very challenging for me. I was shy and found it very difficult to make friends. To those who didn't know me, my shyness came across as stuck up or mean. But to those who knew me, they saw me as kind. Going through the challenge of being misunderstood often affected my self-esteem. I didn't feel like I measured up to other's expectations of me.

As if fitting in with others wasn't challenging enough, it was even more challenging to accept myself. I didn't like my appearance; I struggled to appreciate the color of my skin. Standing next to a fair-skinned person, automatically labeled me as dark-skinned, which made me quite uncomfortable. I viewed my skin color as a flaw because people with lighter skin tones received more time and attention. Back then, my complexion mattered. I didn't realize that my skin color had no bearing on my identity. I was conscious of the way I looked and developed a dependency on being accepted. I viewed myself under an unhealthy lens, subconsciously comparing myself to others and downplaying my value based on their opinions of me.

"If I only had a lighter skin tone, smaller ears, and long *pretty* hair, boys would like me. I would be so popular, and life would be so much better!" Yes— that's what I thought! That unhealthy dialogue was part of my normal. I carried those same insecurities throughout my childhood and viewed myself in light of my imperfections.

My Spiritual Upbringing

Sunday mornings were for church. I remember my mom, who loved to cook, had breakfast ready, which was something I looked forward to. The smell of eggs, bacon, oatmeal, and pancakes used to wake me up. My next phase was the straightening comb. I remember sitting next to the stove in the kitchen, while my mom pressed my hair so that she could give me those pretty styles with ponytails of many colors.

My godmother Trina started this tradition, and everyone at church called me "rainbow," because I had every color barrette you could imagine in my head! I loved staying away on the weekends with my godparents Alex and Trina. One of the things that I remember about staying with them was my favorite meal: baked chicken, string beans, and rice. Even at the age of forty, I can still taste this delicious meal. But more importantly, they helped to push me closer to Christ.

As a little girl, all I could dream of was getting older and receiving the Lord Jesus as my Savior. I was raised in the church, where salvation was reinforced as essential. My siblings and I were taught the importance of having a real relationship with Jesus Christ. Over time, I grew to desire my own personal relationship with Him, although I didn't fully understand what it meant. But because my parents modeled an example of a lifestyle with Jesus Christ as the center, that was the life I desired. I really wanted to be saved.

Growing up, I admired my parents. They were saved and happily married with three children. The life they had was so inspiring. I wanted to be just like them, so I decided to make that my ultimate goal. Even though I was only five years old, I knew that I wanted the life that my parents had. They were my role models. However, I didn't realize that there was a lot more going on under the surface. Things weren't as *perfect* as they seemed. And within that same year, I witnessed an experience that had a rippling effect throughout my childhood into my early adulthood years.

My Breaking Point

At five years old, I hit a breaking point. I walked into the bathroom and saw my mom. Her face, I will never forget. There was a cut on her wrist and a small, metal object. I didn't ask questions. I didn't have time to think. All I knew to do was to call my dad. I was frozen at that moment in time. I don't remember the events after that. My mom received the help that she needed, and she never attempted it again. But at the time, it was like an intense, painful scene in a movie that I will never forget. My innocent world was completely shattered. As a kid, it all seemed perfect. But what I didn't know was that my mom was hurting deeply on the inside.

My mom struggled with suppressed emotions and unresolved issues, causing a mental imbalance. Later in life, she opened up about her challenges, and boldly shared her testimony of God's healing. She overcame depression and had the will to live life to the fullest, as it was not God's will for her to give up on life when times get challenging. It's in those difficult times when God steps in. The Holy Spirit interceded on my mom's behalf, against her attempt to abort God's plan. And after much prayer, I felt the release to share how Jesus Christ restored and healed her entirely through His love and redemptive power.

Overcoming A Mental Illness

Mental illness is real. I've witnessed the evidence of it in my life and my family. As a little girl, I experienced depression, low self-esteem, and suicidal thoughts. I knew that I had an option. At the age of nine, I went into the kitchen and grabbed the biggest knife that I could find and held it to my stomach. I did not penetrate the knife into my stomach, because I was too afraid to. Twenty years later, when I felt that life became too unbearable, I chose to take pills to ease the pain, permanently. At that moment, as a cry for help, I texted my brother and told him that I loved him, but that I was tired. Ten minutes later, my dad came into my apartment, as he only lived minutes away. He had a spare key. Before his arrival, I had consumed several pills. He immediately stopped me in my tracks, and we headed straight to the hospital. I was so concerned about my reputation that I told my dad not to take me because I didn't want it to be on my record. At that moment, I knew that my dad prayed because I didn't feel any effects from the pills that I consumed. Soon after that episode, I decided that it would be the last time that I would take it upon myself to end what God had started.

Although I succumbed to the same generational cycle, God intervened with His infinite power. He broke the cycle of suicide off my family, and I declare this healing over the entire world. Lack of insight, high levels of fear, and unfiltered thoughts and emotions may lead to a destructive path. But you can overcome this! My mom survived it. I survived it. And many family members survived it. So if you've been struggling, you can, too!

Oftentimes, this is a subject that's concealed out of fear and embarrassment. However, at some point, we must be open about our testimony and not be ashamed of communicating it.

"And they overcame him by the blood of the Lamb, and by the word of their testimony..."

— REVELATION 12:11

Someone else's victory is attached to our testimony. Regardless of others' opinions of us, we have to break the silence. Some people may not look at us the same afterward, but we will be free from its bondage. Our silence keeps us stagnant and may block another's forward progression. This truth is a vital part of our story that God can use to help others overcome their struggle.

Overcoming a mental illness may be challenging, but it doesn't have to be our demise.

"He forgives all my sins and heals all my diseases."

— PSALM 103:3

God is a healer. He can heal every ailment and completely restore our health. There is nothing mightier than the healing power of His Word.

The Word of God has a resolution for every matter that we face in life. Most of our battles are rooted in our minds. I liken the mind to a stirring force that causes us to react. Where its rooted can affect the direction we take in life. When our hearts are grounded in the Word of God, we are more likely to move in cadence with the will of God. However, when our hearts are rooted in any other source, we run the risk of operating outside of His will. The Holy Spirit is the governing force that helps us determine if our hearts and minds are God-centered. When all three are in sync, then we can move at a steady pace and make progress. God has a plan, and through finding normalcy in your life, you can choose to come into agreement with what's ahead for you. Trust Him totally with your life!

After many years of prayer and surrender, my mom was able to overcome her depression. She was no longer in bondage to the unhealthy thoughts that tried to imprison her. She was finally able to enjoy her new life with a sound mind. You may be wondering: *What led to this change? How did she become free from the burden of depression?* First, my mom acknowledged that her mental illness was a problem that she couldn't control. She recognized that she could not handle this battle on her own. Second, my mom understood that in order to handle stressful situations properly, she must pray and release it to God. She recognized that the problem wouldn't be resolved as long as it was still in her hands. Third, my mom awaited instruction. She understood that when she completely let go, God would give her the proper insight to handle every burden that was weighing her down. She was obedient to the directive He gave. Obeying His plan freed her from the devastating effects of depression and ultimately produced the results that God desired. Following a lifestyle of prayer and obedience, I was able to witness my mom whole and healed. This experience had a significant impact on my childhood, and its ramifications continued throughout my pre-teen years.

MY PREADOLESCENT YEARS

In Middle School, I would often think to myself, "I just can't wait to get out of Middle School so I can go to High School and take up cosmetology!" I had a genuine passion for practicing cosmetology since the age of nine. I'll never forget the day my dad took me to the hair salon where my mom and cousin worked. Little did I know, I was standing in the same salon that I would later work in, which was first owned by my great aunt and then later, by my cousin!

It wasn't a coincidence that I was standing in that same salon, watching so much creativity take place. I was utterly blown away. I was so amazed by seeing lifeless hair transform into beautiful styles full of body and bounce! I was so intrigued by the creativity and techniques I observed, and I wanted to know how the stylists achieved those results. That day sparked my newfound interest in cosmetology; I was so fascinated by the artistry of hair. At that moment, all I could think about was hair, and I officially decided that I wanted to be a cosmetologist. So, I became my first client in order to perfect my craft. I experimented with various styles and techniques until I became proficient. Soon afterward, my services were in hot demand!

Many family members and friends were impressed with my abilities and wanted me to style their hair, as well! And that's when it all started! I not only took over my own hair care responsibilities, but I was trusted by others to care for theirs. This newfound skill sparked a significant shift in my self-esteem. Although it didn't change the root issues that I struggled with, it helped me push past most of the insecurities I faced as a young girl. During this period, my passion for haircare helped me remain grounded, as I encountered another major breaking point that shook me to my core.

My Breaking Point

During my pre-teen years, I experienced another major breaking point—the separation of my parents. My mom moved out with my oldest brother, and I stayed at home with my dad and my other brother. Growing up as a pre-teen without my mom in the house, deeply affected me.

The separation of my parents was difficult to deal with, but I had to adapt quickly. Life without my mom in the house became my new normal. It took some getting used to, but I had to adjust, despite my lack of understanding. At that time, many things didn't make sense. *How could this happen? Can't y'all just work it out?* I just couldn't wrap my head around all of this.

> "Two are better than one because they have a good return for their labor. If either of them falls down, one can help the other up."
>
> — ECCLESIASTES 4:9-10

I wanted my parents to stay together and resolve their problems. But despite her physical absence, I was grateful to have the opportunity to spend the weekends and summer with her. There were moments, despite the visitation, where the stain of abandonment was still there. This was something that I didn't know how to digest and something that both of my parents did not intentionally do to harm me. This area was not addressed, but I showed the signs of distress. Life was like a pressure kettle that began to boil over in time. My deep feeling of abandonment catalyzed my impending relational challenges.

Experiencing Abandonment

Does the word abandonment sound familiar? Feeling abandoned— the result of someone leaving, renouncing, discarding, disowning, or withdrawing from you— is an emotion that many have experienced. It may be part of *your* normal, but to others, it may be something you've witnessed someone else go through.

Have you ever felt alone? Or, does it feel like someone is always leaving your life? Does the very thought of someone leaving you cause you to make unhealthy decisions in desperation for them to stay? The longing for love, support, and security is natural. And when those desires are threatened, it may influence you to keep someone close, no matter the consequence of that decision.

In life, people come and go. And accepting that reality may be a hard pill to swallow. For whatever reason or rationale, everyone has the propensity for change. However, it's important to remember that God is constant and will forever remain. He is our Father, and He will never leave us.

"For the Lord will not forsake his people; He will not abandon his heritage."

— PSALM 94:14

Despite knowing that, we may place unrealistic expectations on people. We may expect them to stay in our lives forever, not realizing that everyone isn't meant to stay around for the long-haul. So when someone you expected to stay around leaves, it may be detrimental to your heart, thus creating a void. And when there's a void, we may attempt to fill it by finding someone else or engaging in other activities to suppress the pain. However, we must understand that only God is equipped to fill that empty space in our hearts.

But what happens if we experience abandonment over and over again? What if that wound gets deeper and deeper every time we feel abandoned? As a result, we may subconsciously put up a protective wall to keep everyone out. This is similar to how the human body responds to being wounded.

When you have an injury, and something breaks your skin, your body instantly goes into survival mode. The alarm goes off inside, "Hey! You've been hurt. You have to fix this!" In response, your body's natural mechanism will kick in and start working to repair the physical damage that took place. And eventually, the damaged area will heal, and the initial pain will diminish. The problem, however, is that our hearts store information differently. Therefore, we may continue to be in bondage to a painful memory, long after the situation happened, whereas, our bodies don't keep score of the past. And because it's sometimes hard to let go of the painful memories in our heart, it can cause an emotional scar.

Nurturing your pain can lead to emotional scarring. When we experience emotional suffering, it may eventually morph into a heavy weight and become tethered to our memories. We may begin to store its pain and bury ourselves in a pile of accumulated trauma. If we aren't careful, we may respond to unrelated issues in an unhealthy manner due to being on edge from unresolved emotional distress.

Imagine if your heart was a bag full of pain that was carried around every day. And when something comes along that triggers that bag of pain, it not only affects one issue, but it stirs up everything that's in the bag. *Why?* This is because everything inside is vulnerable. Despite the situation being part of the past, the unresolved pain and memory remain present. Imagine a calloused heart that has been scarred so much that nothing or no one can penetrate. This was not God's original plan, but He has a resolution for the problem before it began: a new heart— a heart of flesh!

"I will give you a new heart and put a new spirit in you; I will remove from you your heart of stone and give you a heart of flesh."

— EZEKIEL 36:26

Effects of Abandonment

Pain doesn't discriminate. It knows no age, race, or gender. It can affect anyone at any time. It can be equally as hard for adults as it for children. The significant difference is that the brain of a child is still developing, and processing an influx of complicated emotions can be quite overwhelming.

Although children are not responsible for the challenges their parents face, they may experience trauma that suggests otherwise. They may feel guilty for causing this disruption and become traumatized by the sudden change. All they want is normalcy.

In houses of dysfunction, the embodiment of a mother and father is healthy. This isn't to suggest that dysfunction is healthy, but to emphasize that God established the home's structure to be a certain way. God intended the family unit to operate with both a mother and father, as both genders play critical roles in the upbringing of their children.

Parents aren't perfect, as mistakes are inevitable. As a parent, we must pray and follow God's leading. He may impart to us certain truths to help us make wise decisions, but conceal other matters that may require us to stand still and fully place our trust in Him. And although we may think we're doing the right thing, the effects of our decisions may not go as planned. This could harm our children and affect how they live the rest of their lives. Therefore, it's essential to go back to the beginning to uncover the root issues that may have altered the trajectory of their lives.

Overcoming Abandonment

The day my parents separated, my entire world changed. I was not used to life without her in the home. The comfort of having both parents home was my normal; it was the normalcy I was accustomed to. This forced me to neglect what was familiar and sort through an overwhelming amount of complicated emotions. But because it was too much for me to manage, I suppressed them. I didn't know that I could talk to someone about my experiences. If I had a counselor, I believe things would've been much different for me. But I had to learn that this was a part of my process— *my normal.* God turned it around for my good! This was necessary, and it was the driving force for my next lifetime decision.

Later in life, I became a counselor. Being in this profession expanded my understanding of how to manage complex emotions. I often reflected on my experience as a child, wishing I had the opportunity to express my feelings and walk through the transition of my parents' separation in a healthy way.

But was that God's plan? Was that my normal? Did God allow me to struggle through the transition of my parents' separation so that I could share my journey of healing with others thirty-one years later? Many times, we don't understand the *whys* of life until later on. But at that moment, we are better equipped to handle that truth with clarity and maturity.

Until I received clarity from God, I struggled with not understanding why. My confusion manifested itself through intense grief, depression, and isolation. As an attempt to ease my pain, I observed other families who had both parents at home and desperately wished for the same. But no one knew this. No one really understood how I felt in my heart and emotions. On the outside, was a forced smile. But on the inside, was a deep feeling of abandonment. I struggled with this pain for so long until I finally decided that it was time for a change. It was time for me to heal.

Declaration of Healing from Abandonment

My Beloved Father, in the Name of Jesus, I declare freedom-- **right now** — for whoever may be dealing with or have dealt with the pain of abandonment, and are unsure if they are truly free from its bondage. I declare— **right now**— in the matchless Name of Jesus, that whom the Son sets free is free indeed! So, do not be entangled again with the yoke of bondage!

God's divine presence is falling upon you now. Receive your healing from abandonment and know that you have been adopted into the family of God. Today, forgive those who left your life and release them to your Father. God said that He would never leave you nor forsake you. You will no longer walk through life feeling rejected or abandoned. You are whole and healed.

Embrace every season that God is taking you through because everyone can't go with you. Divine connections and healthy relationships are being released. Ordained relationships that have been severed are being restored.

In the Name of Jesus, be healed and restored! Amen.

Embracing Forgiveness

Years later, I mustered up the nerve to approach my mom. I shared my true feelings about her departure and how it impacted my life. Despite my honesty, I was intentional about not blaming her or my dad for separating, as my sole purpose was to open up my heart, not to make accusations. During our time together, I expressed my lack of understanding surrounding the dynamics of what took place. I conveyed my perspective as a child who witnessed her mom packing up her things and moving out without understanding why. I communicated the feeling of abandonment I experienced as a result of it, and how I felt alone. I wanted her to understand everything that was going on in my heart. I realized that I carried around the weight of this hurt for years and needed to release this pain from my heart. To do that, I had to forgive my mom for a decision she made that was not intended to harm me. And after I forgave her, a beautiful thing took place. Not only was my heart able to heal, but our relationship was reconciled. Our relationship grew stronger, as an offense no longer hindered it.

In addition, my parents demonstrated their ability to forgive and move forward. Despite their final decision to divorce, they were able to model both love and forgiveness. My dad still cared for my mom and made sure that he was there for her if she ever needed anything. Witnessing their ability to forgive each other and still be friends without animosity or resentment was a life-changing blessing for me to experience. I experienced the significant impact of learning to forgive, receiving healing, and releasing hurt in exchange for the joy of the Lord. Therefore, I desire to extend that same guidance to all who may feel stuck in the same dilemma.

If there is someone you are holding contempt in your heart, please release them right now. You will experience such freedom and joy when you can let them go.

Prayer of Forgiveness

My Beloved Father, I choose to confront this feeling of resentment towards (*insert name*) because of (*state the past hurt or concern*), which has caused me to build barriers around my heart that wouldn't allow You to enter. So now, I pray for healing and restoration in my heart. I forgive (*insert name*) and myself, in the Name of Jesus. Amen!

With God, all things are possible to those that believe. It was not my place to know all of the details, but it is my mission to encourage other married couples to pray together, study the Word of God together, and to everything in unity, giving no space for the enemy. Seek wise counsel for matters that you cannot work through with amongst yourselves. Don't give up until you both have exhausted every possibility to salvage the marriage. Marriage is honorable, as it foreshadows Christ's marriage to the church. Two are better than one, and it's a beautiful thing when two people come together in harmony to walk out destiny together. This relationship not only embodies the relationship between Christ and the church but also models a healthy lifestyle for children to follow. I was so glad to see that my parents were able to truly forgive each other and model love. They remained friends for several years, until they both transitioned, three years apart.

MY TEENAGE YEARS

At this stage in my life, everything changed. It was the time when I lost my innocence. That was a significant turning point for me. This period marked a major shift in my life.

In Middle School, I was always curious about the conversations I overheard by my peers. They talked about their sexual encounters in class! I couldn't believe it; this was Middle School! This was a time when we're beginning to learn more about our emotions and our bodies. Most children are going through puberty, and if not properly channeled, their emotions can lead them down the wrong path. Without the guidance of adults or mentors to explain things to you in detail, it's hard to know what to do with those complex emotions. I will never forget what my parents, my pastor, and the religious leaders around me used to say. I was told that it is good to wait until you are married to have sex. I didn't understand the depth of why that was so important, but it caused me to be awakened in ways that I was not ready for.

God's Law Reveals Our Sin

"Well then, am I suggesting that the law of God is sinful? Of course not! In fact, it was the law that showed me my sin. I would never have known that coveting is wrong if the law had not said, 'You must not covet.' But sin used this command to arouse all kinds of covetous desires within me! If there were no law, sin would not have that power. At one time, I lived without understanding the law. But when I learned the command not to covet, for instance, the power of sin came to life, and I died. So I discovered that the law's commands, which were supposed to bring life, brought spiritual death instead. Sin took advantage of those commands and deceived me; it used the commands to kill me. But still, the law itself is holy, and its commands are holy and right and good."

— ROMANS 7:7-12

Acknowledging that an action is wrong, but without the proper understanding, is a dangerous formula. After receiving the command not to engage in unlawful behaviors, it's important to understand why it's not appropriate and how to overcome any habit that may have surfaced. Therefore, it's essential that Biblical application is applied, as it will provide the wisdom needed to overcome any urges or habits. Adopting the mindset of Christ, while receiving a consistent stream sound doctrine will assist you in maintaining discipline, which can be applied to every area of your life.

Soon after that experience, I thought to myself: "Okay, so I've done it! I'm a woman now!" I felt like I finally understood what everyone was talking about. And now, I did not feel left out. There were many people close to my age that were not virgins. And even though I fit in— or so I thought— I didn't realize how precious that gift was until several years down the line.

My Breaking Point

As a teenager, I hit another breaking point. After I received Christ as my Savior, I realized the emotional trauma caused by losing my innocence. I discovered that I made a huge mistake. I took on pain that wasn't meant for me to handle at that young age. This caused me to heavily engage in substance abuse to numb the pain, as I wasn't mature or capable enough to handle the consequences of my actions.

Becoming spiritually one with someone that you aren't married to is a major challenge to work through! Not knowing how to spiritually detox will cause significant emotional instability. I wondered if every relationship I entered into with the opposite sex was "the one." *Is this the guy that is going to love me the way I need to be loved? And at the age of thirteen and fourteen, how would I know what to look for? Would I be able to recognize true love if I experienced it?*

Children Need Direction

As a child, our first example of receiving love is from our parents. And whether it's expressed with balance or dysfunction, God has a solution. Therefore, it is only in our relationship with our Heavenly Father that we can experience the purest form of love. In relationship with Him, we can experience His love and share it with others, as we walk in His Spirit. When we are connected to Him, the power of His love can flow to our children, family members, and even those we don't have close relationships with. If we can properly distribute love in our own home, that can equip us to disburse love to others we don't know.

Parents, guardians, and mentors must pray, to be led by God regarding how to speak to children about specific topics that are difficult, yet necessary to discuss. This includes the issue of sexuality. Children need to know that their bodies are the temple of the Holy Spirit and that it should be kept sacred and protected.

"Or do you not know that your body is the temple of the Holy Spirit who is in you, whom you have from God, and you are not your own? For you were bought at a price; therefore glorify God in your body and in your spirit, which are God's."

— 1 CORINTHIANS 6:19-20

There's Nothing New Under the Sun

Raising teenagers during this phase of their lives may be quite challenging, regardless of what was instilled in them since birth. This is arguably the most rebellious stage of their lives. At this point, they are learning right from wrong, and are challenged to use that information to make the right decisions. They may have done some things right by trial and error and assumed that they now have everything covered. They may look at their parents as old and outdated, thinking things have changed since they were young. But the reality is, it hasn't changed. My dad used to quote Ecclesiastes 1:9 all the time: "There is nothing new under the sun."

"What has been will be again, what has been done will be done again; there is nothing new under the sun."

— ECCLESIASTES 1:9

As a teenager, I thought I was getting over on my dad. But little did I know, he was always a thousand steps ahead of me!

During this time, I wanted to try my hand at recreational drugs. But thankfully, that idea was short-lived. And to this day, I'm glad that as soon as that door was opened, it was immediately shut. I had many issues as a little girl with bronchitis, and often I went to the hospital for breathing treatments because my bronchial tubes were small. Later, I was grateful for having that issue, as it stopped me from what could have been a lifelong, deadly habit. People say smoking is fun, but my experience was quite different. The first time I tried smoking, it was fun and exciting. But the second time, when I smoked with a friend, I felt like I was about to die. I could not breathe, and I prayed so hard for the high to wear off because I didn't want to go to the hospital and face my dad's disappointment in me. But I thank God for prayer— which worked quite quickly, might I add! Shortly after the prayer I released, I could breathe. I was so happy and thankful that God saved my life. When I got home, I laid down immediately and reminisced about the blessing that took place.

Reflecting on everything today, I am very grateful for this learning experience. I am thankful for the discipline I received from my dad during my times of disobedience, which has groomed me into the woman that I am today.

Your Life Has Purpose

As a teenager in high school, all I could think about was growing up, getting a job, and getting my own place. Those were my goals toward achieving my own independence. I wasn't concerned with why God put me here. But as a parent today, I see things from a different perspective. I truly understand the importance of imparting and instructing your children to focus on why God has put them here. If you ask them questions at a young age, you may be surprised by the answers you receive concerning their future.

At the age of eleven, my son told me five things he wanted to become when he gets older. I was so impressed by what he shared.

> When I get older, I want to become:
> 1. A Barbershop Owner
> 2. A Pianist
> 3. A Video Gamer
> 4. An Author
> 5. A Child of God

The fact that he knows what he wants at this age is mind-boggling to me, as I have been asking him this question for months. So, as his parents, my husband and I have made sure that we invest in each area of his gifting. And whether or not he decides to do all or a few of what he mentioned on his list, he has our prayers and support. I am just very proud of what he shared. We know that he will be a strong leader and an advocate for those that don't have the boldness to speak up for themselves. He will be a helper to many and ultimately a soul winner for Christ. And with his God-given focus and determination, I know that he will achieve everything God has in store for him. By having this determination early in life, it will help shape his normalcy, as he transitions into adulthood.

MY ADULTHOOD YEARS

As an adult, I didn't understand why my life was so painful. That's when I pleaded to God: *Why can't my life just be normal?* During my adulthood years, I experienced three major breaking points. Those experiences changed my outlook on life and served as a testimony to help others overcome their challenges.

My First Breaking Point

Marriage is something that most women look forward to. Everything about the wedding— picking out the dress, choosing bridesmaids, and planning the honeymoon— is exciting and truly something to look forward to! I was in love with the idea of being married, but was not prepared for everything that came with it! I did not know that the foundation of what was being built had to be stable.

At the age of twenty-five, I went through a divorce. At that age, most women get married, have a family, and live happily ever after. But that was not quite my story, as my marriage only lasted one year. After experiencing physical and verbal abuse, I knew that if I continued this marriage, it would have led to years of pain and disappointment.

After suffering from the miscarriage of my first baby boy, I finally decided to leave. This was devastating because I never thought in a million years that I would be divorced within two years of getting married. My dad was able to walk me down the aisle, and it was the most memorable moment ever. But sometimes, the choices we make in our lives can leave us scarred and broken, taking many years to recover.

I didn't realize the trauma that my previous marriage and divorce caused until I entered into other relationships. That pain affected me for years. Sometimes, we may be in denial about how hurt we were, but our bodies don't lie. They have a natural defense mechanism that tells us we're fine, as long as we keep living and going on with our normal schedule. So when we move on to new relationships— five, ten, or even fifteen years later— we experience the effects of letting the ingredients in a pot of soup settle. As soon as we start stirring the pot, all of the ingredients from the bottom mix together, and then we get the gist of how the soup tastes. So when you begin a new relationship, after coming out of a traumatic one, all of the emotions that were lying dormant may get stirred up, forcing the new person to eat the soup of your past. All of the ingredients from the soup of your past relationship was brought into your new relationship. And now, the new person has become the recipient of unresolved hurt and pain. Is this fair— no! Did you purposely do this to cause harm to the other person— *no*! Can you fix it without ruining the relationship— *yes*!

Seek Wise Counsel

To combat the effects of trauma, it is necessary to incorporate therapy and prayer for healing. Truly, it was my relationship with God, consistent prayers, and fasting that got me through my darkest days. And as an advocate of counseling and therapy for healing, I firmly believe that God has blessed us with wise counselors to help us walk through challenging situations. We just have to accept that sometimes we need help. And as the Bible says, there is safety in an environment of advisers.

"Where no counsel is, the people fall: but in the multitude of counselors, there is safety."

— PROVERBS 11:14

Oftentimes, God will lead you to someone to share the truth of your emotions in order to receive wise counsel. Sometimes, there may be situations where you feel like you can't go to your friends for help.

You may be:

1. Uncomfortable, as there may not be an emotional connection with them on that level
2. Turned off by a previous encounter, where you received a response that didn't sit well with you
3. Prideful about exposing your vulnerability, so your friends won't see you in a particular light
4. Unaccustomed to telling people how you honestly feel

Regardless of the reason, our responses to how we deal with people are generally centered on cultural differences and family core values. In some family settings, you may have been told to keep things quiet and not share your business. So, you may have grown up being private about certain things that needed to be shared. Nonetheless, we must be cautious about who we share our private information with. The Scripture above reminds us that safety is found in the company of counselors. That environment is a safe place to share our feelings without feeling judged and enables us to feel comfortable being who we are while receiving sound advice with love.

You Can Live Again

Ultimately, God is the only One that can take a broken heart, mend the broken pieces, and construct a renewed heart. With Christ, you can receive a fresh start. You may have thought you were all mangled, no good, and completely ruined. But with God, He can turn the whole situation around. He can allow you to live again! But you must ask yourself, *are you ready to live again?* Sometimes you may have to pick up the pieces and start all over! It is not the end of your journey; it is not the end of your fight! It's not the end of your story; it's the end of this chapter! And I am living proof that you can start all over and live again!

After my divorce, I had to start all over again; I needed a new job, car, and identity. I felt like I lost myself in my one-year marriage because everything that I thought was real was a smokescreen. This was a hard pill to swallow because I was so naive to the real world and how things operated. I was living in a fantasy world, and I needed someone to wake me up to the reality of how things were. Life really shook me. It was a reality check— a wakeup call! I learned a valuable lesson from that experience. I understood that I needed to consult God about every step that I take in my life, as it will save me years of recovery and regret.

Overcome By Forgiveness

In life, we must be able to understand both past and present situations from a different perspective. Despite the experience of something traumatic, we must be willing to understand that some things weren't intentional. People often respond to others in a way that dictates their response to something that previously happened to them. People don't always intend to hurt you. But if their actions were considered beforehand, they may have avoided an adverse reaction. Oftentimes, this is where regret steps in, which can lead to a cycle of unfiltered emotions. In turn, we may learn that what happened to us, whether intentional or unintentional, was a result of a flawed character built on falsehood. And that's why it's essential to receive God as our Father and reclaim our true identity and forgive others for their mistakes.

Choose to walk in forgiveness, knowing that the person who hurt you was probably wounded, too. Pray and release your offender. Consider reconciliation, if God leads you to do so. Or, simply forgive the individual and move on. If you choose to forgive and move forward without reconciliation, walk away with the understanding that people generally hurt others from a place of unresolved hurt. And most of their actions may have been based on what they deem to be culturally correct, as someone with an unhealthy perspective may have influenced them. In general, most of our responses are birthed out of what we know and understand to be true. We tend to make decisions based on our level of maturity at certain stages in our lives. Understanding that principle may help you in the process of forgiveness.

Lessons Learned

Sharing your life story does not mean you have to deliver it from a negative perspective. What you share should come from a place of transparency and healing. For me, sharing my story was therapeutic. As I began to dig deeper into what the Holy Spirit led me to write, more profound healing took place. While sharing my story of finding my normal, I was able to see that all of my mistakes, failures, and victories were lessons that molded me into the woman I am today.

My story was birthed from a place of trying to find out the answers to why my life turned out the way that it did. I would often ask the question: *what influenced me to go down the paths that I traveled?* Realizing that most of my actions were based upon generational tendencies that were passed down, I wanted to break free from that cycle of living. I recognized that this was my normal, but that it didn't have to be the end of my story. God was simply molding me into a change agent for others, while carrying me gracefully through the transitions of life.

Transitioning from a culture of stagnation into one of freedom was a major shock! Eventually, the effects of the shock diminished. I looked up one day and noticed that change wasn't that bad at all. I could now see that it was a healthy part of my growth. I learned to embrace the changes in my life and let the *shocks* in life awaken my true self. I was finally living life alive and free.

Now, I live life with no regrets, as it has been a journey well-lived. And as God continues to take me through adventure after adventure, this is not the end of my journey. Greater is coming! Trust God and believe that there is new life for you!

So, to those who have experienced divorce, understand that there is hope for you! Divorce is not the end of your life or your love story. You can love again. Take back your life and live again! Be healed and be set free! Receive God's love! That chapter is over; begin a new one. Don't be afraid to start again. Embrace what God has ahead for you! You are not a victim! Walk in victory! Freedom is yours!

Prayer of Healing from Divorce

My Beloved Father, I thank You for the genuine love that you have shown me throughout my life. Today, I choose to receive my healing from all of the lies spoken about my identity that built up walls around my heart. I declare that— **today**— these walls are coming down! The power of God destroys every lie, and Your truth about me shall prevail! I declare healing from all of the physical, emotional, and verbal abuse experienced throughout my lifetime. I declare that whom the Son sets free is free indeed. And today, I choose freedom, in Jesus' Name. Amen.

My Second Breaking Point

After my divorce, I experienced another breaking point. I got pregnant, and it was very challenging. I didn't understand why my pregnancy with my son Joshua was so difficult, but it all makes sense now.

Due to the miscarriage in my previous marriage, my current doctor mentioned that I would need a cervical cerclage if I ever decided to conceive again. This procedure treats cervical weakness by reinforcing the cervix during pregnancy and helps to ensure a full-term pregnancy. To my surprise, after my first trimester, my same doctor assured me that a cerclage was no longer needed. However, two and a half months later, he regretted making that decision.

At five and a half months pregnant, I begin to have contractions. I pleaded with God to let my son stay in my womb until he was fully developed. With prayers, along with the assistance of the doctors, I was put on bed rest for the remainder of my pregnancy. I was given an IV with medicine to stop my contractions. I kept thinking to myself: *is this happening as a result of my sin?* Later, I realized that my son was God's blessing to me, regardless of how he was conceived. God had a plan in mind when his conception took place. Before he was conceived, God knew Joshua and sent him here through me.

The fact that I was about to embark on another journey of bringing a baby into the world, after having a miscarriage, was such a beautiful thing. It was as if I was given another opportunity to carry my child full-term, and maybe this time, my situation would be better! The harsh reality of it all was that I conceived my child out of wedlock, and I was an elder in the church. I was so ashamed and regretted this decision, but I found peace in God in the midst of it all. It was a rollercoaster ride of happiness and shame, and all I could do was pray that my emotional distress did not affect my unborn child. My parents were excited and very supportive, along with other friends and family. I repented, and my relationship with God was clear, but in the sight of those that carried a religious, condemning mindset, I was damaged goods. There were times when I felt like it was over. Sometimes, instead of encouragement and restoration, I received looks that made me want to go and hide.

FINDING NORMAL

Five months into my pregnancy, I was granted the time that I needed by myself. Even though it felt like torture, in the beginning, I later realized that I needed that time to spend with God. Though it felt like I had a lack of support, I had to accept that this was my choice. I realized that some people don't have the ability to look beyond your mistakes and assure you that there is hope for your future.

"Dear brothers and sisters, if another believer is overcome by some sin, you who are godly should gently and humbly help that person back onto the right path. And be careful not to fall into the same temptation yourself."

— GALATIANS 6:1

Knowing that everyone may not humbly help us back onto the right path can cause us to hold bitterness towards them in our hearts. Regardless of the situation, we must learn to forgive them and no longer hold others hostage to the expectations they didn't meet. God truly healed my heart of this pain and helped me learn to forgive.

During this season, God reminded me of His miracle-working power. He kept my son in my womb until he was thirty-seven weeks developed and reminded me of the miracle of my conception. While in my previous marriage, I was told that I was infertile and would never be able to get pregnant due to an overactive thyroid. Despite the doctor's verdict, I prayed and was pregnant a month later. Three months later, I had a miscarriage because of the weakness of my cervix. Regardless of the miscarriage, the miracle was that I could get pregnant. God was showing me that He had the power to open my womb. And years later, my son Josh was birthed.

At the age of two, doctors pronounced that my son had a developmental delay. Many people stated that he was autistic. But despite what they said, I prayed and anointed him every day. I stood on the Word of God over Joshua's life. I had the support and prayers of many during this time. It took much prayer and the spiritual strength of others throughout this journey. Every day, I spoke over Joshua and declared God's Word, and it gradually began to manifest.

At the age of four, Joshua attended Head Start. He was smarter than his entire class! His teachers frequently pulled me aside to tell me how intelligent he was. At that moment, I knew that God turned it all around and wanted me to share this testimony of His grace with others.

Throughout the journey of his academic success, Joshua's performance has exceeded my prayers. And this year, he will be publishing his first book, *The Coolson's Kids: The Family of Peace*, so stay tuned! Now more than ever, I can confidently say: *What the devil meant for evil, God worked it out for his good*!

Nurture Your Promise

At this juncture, I've been able to share my story with women who've experienced a similar story. It is truly a blessing to encourage others to hold on to the promises of God. Joshua is God's manifested promise to me. He is my miracle baby! I am so blessed to have him. And just like the story of Hannah, I've dedicated Joshua back to God.

"And she made this vow: "O Lord of Heaven's Armies, if you will look upon my sorrow and answer my prayer and give me a son, then I will give him back to you. He will be yours for his entire lifetime, and as a sign that he has been dedicated to the Lord, his hair will never be cut."

— 1 SAMUEL 1:11

As parents, it is our responsibility to make sure that we dedicate our children back to God. We must pour into them all that God gives us to give to them. It is our responsibility to equip them with all of the necessary things to move forward in their lives by God's divine help and instructions. As parents, we don't take that lightly.

My husband has been very instrumental in the spiritual growth and development of our son. Not only did he teach him how to bounce a ball and ride a bike, but he showed him the importance of living a life that is pleasing to God. He taught him the fundamentals of life and how to be a strong man, while adhering to Biblical values. And as a result, our son Joshua has confidence and knows who he is.

It truly warms my heart to look back on everything that took place. God always comes through. He never forgets His promise! Truly, He deserves all of the glory and praise for the wonderful things that He has done!

My Third Breaking Point

Following the birth of my son, I experienced intense emotional distress. I was in my 30s, and things became unbearable for me to handle. I couldn't deal with any more sudden changes in my life. Anything that shifted suddenly would put the brakes on my joy, peace, and consistency. I asked a friend of mine to take me to the hospital to admit myself. I wanted to be medicated and sleep my life away. The thought of having to cope with the pain and repercussions of my decisions, along with things I had no control over was too much, or so I thought.

As a result of expressing how I felt, I was directed to the psych ward. It was not at all what I imagined it to be. The colors of the wall were gray, and the lights were dim. I was directed to walk down a long, cold hallway that led to a room with other people waiting in it to see the doctors for an evaluation. But because it was nighttime, the doctor was gone and would not be able to see patients until the morning. I thought to myself, "Great! Now I have to sit here all night!" They offered me something to help me sleep, but I declined. The Lord said to me, "You don't belong here!" and I wholeheartedly agreed with Him. But there was one problem! Based on the hospital's rules, once you are admitted, you cannot leave until the doctor releases you after being evaluated. Despite knowing the rules, I knew what God said, so I asked the lady there, "Can I please leave?" I even assured her that I wouldn't harm myself. She said, "I'm not supposed to do this, but I'll let you leave." After hearing that, I was so relieved! I walked out of that place, realizing that I was better off at home. Going there made me feel worse than when I arrived.

Months later, I discovered a house for women who suffered from mental instabilities. I packed up some clothes and went to visit the house. When I walked in, I did not feel comfortable. The place was not tidy. I left and went back home within twenty minutes of my arrival. I knew I didn't belong there.

I was confused. I thought I was doing the right thing. I made two attempts to seek help, but neither option was for me. I just knew there had to be another solution. And there was! That day, I found rest in the arms of God. I cried out and asked Him to free me from myself. It was apparent that I didn't know what decision to make or which route to take. So, I remained faithful to what I knew. I continued to attend church and adjusted my posture. I practiced trading in my sorrows for the joy of the Lord. I put on the garment of praise for the spirit of heaviness, and I sought wise counsel from those equipped to help me press through. Recovery from trauma requires perseverance and determination. Even when you don't see or feel any signs of change, you must be determined to keep moving forward.

Begin Again

Today, I am 40 years old, with a wonderful husband and an exuberant son. And years ago, I decided to live again! I am living life in God's perfect will— an experience that I didn't feel was possible! I felt like I made so many mistakes that weren't recoverable. The hardest part of it was learning how to forgive myself and move forward, while allowing myself time to recuperate. But it was possible. I was able to forgive, heal, and trust God throughout the next phase of my journey!

So today, let's begin a new chapter in your life. Grab your journal, write today's date, and start planning! Start living! Get in your mind that you will not allow your past to ruin your future. It's time to pick up the pieces and move forward!

REFLECT/ JOURNAL

RESOURCES FOR CHAPTER TWO

Refer to the 30 Day Devotional
Day 2: "Mind the Matter"
(*Available November 2021*)

Refer to Strategies of Finding Normal
"Overcoming Heartbreak & Abuse"

*Let's do this exercise
before you begin Chapter 2...*

It's time to push forward and let the past go!

Get a piece of paper. Think of a time in your life—even if it's right now! Write that moment down (past or present). Then, say this prayer.

God, "Therefore if any man be in Christ, he is a new creature: old things are passed away; behold, all things are become new." — 2 Corinthians 5:17

RESOURCES FOR CHAPTER TWO

Prayer of Salvation

My Beloved Father, I acknowledge that I need Your help in this life on earth and that I cannot do anything without You. I realize that You had a resolution for the fall of mankind that started with Adam, but I thank You that the story didn't stop there! So, today, I acknowledge that I have sinned, and I ask You to forgive me of them all.

I believe that You sent Your son Jesus Christ to die as a sinless sacrifice so that I can be free from sin and have a relationship with You.

I receive my free gift of eternal life today. And I receive You perseveration and guidance through the person of the Holy Spirit, to guide me through the rest of this life.

In the Name of Jesus, Amen.

RESOURCES FOR CHAPTER TWO

Now, speak to the situation...

Now, I speak an ending to this situation— any ties to any past hurts that have lingered and tried to stay connected to me all the way up until this point. I am announcing my departure from the situation.

As a prophetic symbol of faith, I will take the scissors and cut all ties from my past to my future. They will be destroyed and I will walk into my new life as God's new creation: *reborn, renewed,* and *revived.*

So, now take a pair of scissors and cut the paper in half. Ball it up, throw it in the trash, and say: "It is finished!"

When Jesus said it was finished, He gave up the ghost and returned back to be seated at the right Hand of His Father.

God wants our way to diminish and His way to be our way of living. When we are seated, we are hidden and protected in the world, but not of the world; we live in an ascended place.

2

PICK UP THE PIECES

Many of us can say that we have been broken in some way. We may have put our confidence in someone or been disappointed with plans that did not work out the way we thought. This is something that happens to everyone. So, no matter where you are in your life, you may have experienced brokenness in some way. But what I love about God, as according to the word of God, this is when He is the closest to us.

> "The Lord is near to the brokenhearted; He saves the contrite in spirit."
>
> — PSALM 34:18

Situations that you've been through may have left you hopeless. And you may think to yourself, *"Why even try?"* You may feel as though every time you attempt to move forward in your life that there is something in your way that's blocking you from making progress. Have you thought something like this at some point in your life? This is what you call *normal*. You may have wondered why you can't have a normal life, but what I just described is normal.

As a little child, we start with a clean slate. It is our parents' (or caretakers') responsibility to make sure we learn everything we need to know that's foundational. We must learn to walk, talk, and understand the difference between right and wrong. At that stage in our lives, it's the responsibility of others to take care of us and lead the way, setting a firm foundation for us to build upon. However, some children aren't privy to positive influences at the beginning of their lives. But in some way, God may allow someone to come along to impart to them the fundamentals of how to live a successful life. So, it may not always come from the people we expect it to come from. Despite how it's done, God has a sure way of getting the right information to us at the right time, so that we can get to our destiny with the right essentials.

We have to take advantage of the information that we're given and use it to have the victorious life that God intended. Success does not mean you will have a life free of hurt and pain, but rather, you will experience a life full of blessings, joy, peace, hope, and some pain— to bring out the beauty of life itself. When you consider a plant, it's evident that its foundation is soil. Soil may be messy, but out of it comes something profitable. It's vital to appreciate times of pain and disappointment, as it helps us appreciate the times of sunshine. We should also embrace those valuable lessons learned to help others become better individuals and live a productive life.

Sometimes life may break you down to the point where you feel like you can't be repaired. Some people walk through life experiencing disappointment after disappointment, and never receive healing. They may get to a point where they are so broken down that it's damaging to their health. And that could cause them to lose effectiveness in their lives and hinder any significant progress. It could come in between their relationships with family and friends, but most importantly, their relationship with God. At this point, it's important to be honest with yourself and admit that you are broken. Admit that you feel like you've left a piece of yourself with the person you experienced trauma with. Once you are honest with yourself, decide that it's time to go back and pick up the pieces.

You may be wondering how to do this, as it was so painful dealing with those situations of the past, and you may not want to revisit it. But the truth of the matter is, you have to. There is a part of you that is damaged that needs to be repaired. So, you have to go back to that place where you left a piece of you and allow God's divine Hand to repair you. He may send people to pray with you and to give you godly wisdom to make it through the situation. He will orchestrate the healing process. And when you are restored, then you will be able to pick up that piece of you that was broken.

There may be a part of you that likes to have fun, loves to be around people, or loves to go to the gym and work out. There may be parts of you that you left at that broken place, and you didn't realize it. Wherever you are in your life, it's never too late to be restored. Whether you left those broken pieces in your childhood years, teenage years, or adulthood years, they can be recovered.

But are some pieces worth picking up or should they be left where you found them? Some things are better left alone. Instead of picking it up to nurture it back to health or to see if there is any hope of resolution, sometimes it's best to let it be. In those cases, just letting it be may be a healthy resolve. Other parties may not be willing to make peace and come to a compromise. And because we cannot control their actions, it may be best to approach them later or permanently leave the situation alone. Upon prayer, God will bring the clarity needed and instruct you on what to do. He may lead you to forgive, be healed, and move forward. Or, He may reconnect you with the person after the healing takes place. We are not to make that decision on our own without His guidance.

REFLECT/ JOURNAL

RESOURCES FOR CHAPTER THREE

Refer to the 30 Day Devotional
Day 25: "Take the Time to Heal"
(*Available November 2021*)

*Before you begin Chapter 3,
understand how wounds heal...*

A wound is a break or opening in the skin. Your skin protects your body from germs. When the skin is broken, even during surgery, germs can enter and cause infection. Wounds often occur because of an accident or injury.

Wounds heal in stages. The smaller the wound, the quicker it will heal. The larger or deeper the wound, the longer it takes to heal. When you get a cut, scrape, or puncture, the wound will bleed.

RESOURCES FOR CHAPTER THREE

- The blood will start to clot within a few minutes or less and stop the bleeding.

- The blood clots dry and form a scab, which protects the tissue underneath from germs.

- The wound becomes slightly swollen, red or pink, and tender.

- You also may see some clear fluid oozing from the wound. This fluid helps clean the area.

- Blood vessels open in the area, so blood can bring oxygen and nutrients to the wound. Oxygen is essential for healing.

- White blood cells help fight infection from germs and begin to repair the wound.

Tissue growth and rebuilding occur next.

RESOURCES FOR CHAPTER THREE

- Over the next 3 weeks or so, the body repairs broken blood vessels and new tissue grows.

- Red blood cells help create collagen, which are tough, white fibers that form the foundation for new tissue.

- The wound starts to fill in with new tissue, called granulation tissue.

- New skin begins to form over this tissue.

- As the wound heals, the edges pull inward, and the wound gets smaller.

- A scar forms and the wound becomes stronger.

After reading all of what it takes to heal a physical wound, just know that God is healing your heart of past wounds that sometimes grow deeper roots because we have held on to them for so long.

RESOURCES FOR CHAPTER THREE

1. Cleanse the wound.
2. Allow the wound to breathe. Take some time to pray and release to God. A counselor or pastor can also help you through this process.
3. Fight the infection. This process won't be easy; it will take some effort.
4. Form your new mindset, as you have a new perception of the matter.
5. Embrace the change. Before you know it, the wound will be smaller and may soon fade away.
6. Tell the story. You make have a scar, but this is just a reminder of what happened and how you made it through the process of healing. There's no more pain! So, tell the story so that others can overcome, too!

Today, choose the healing that God has for you!

Information retrieved from:
Medline Plus
"How Wounds Heal"
https://medlineplus.gov/ency/patientinstructions/000741.htm

3

BE HEALED

*O*ftentimes, we find that the problems we've faced in life can become our weakness. Unintentionally, we can pass them on to our children, or those around us, causing them to succumb to the effects of what we have experienced. The ones that are closest to us may become casualties of our war. It's time for us to heal so that we don't always struggle with the same battle and negatively affect those closest to us.

"Give your burdens to the Lord, and he will take care of you. He will not permit the godly to slip and fall."

— PSALM 55:22

Sometimes, it can be hard to hide where you are in your life. You may not want to project what you are feeling on the inside to others. There could be times when you wake up in the morning and not be content with your life. Because of this, you may not feel like interacting with others, but do so anyway, just to be kind. You may be hurting on the inside and struggling with something you've been trying to conquer your entire life. The life that you have in mind may not be the life you currently see. Therefore, you may experience unpleasant feelings and project them onto those you come in contact with. You may try to hide those feelings for a season, but how you feel may become apparent. Most of the time, it may affect the ones you care for the most. God may be sending people to mentor you, but your actions may push your help away. So, we must submit those feelings to God and seek Him about what to do next.

DAVID & THE AMALEKITES

As we reflect on the Amalekites' story, we can see that David was devastated after the Amalekites destroyed Ziklag, a Judean village, and everything they owned. They also took as hostage their villagers' women and some of David's children. David sought the counsel of the Lord regarding what to do next. Despite the strength of the enemy, David trusted God to have his back. David defeated the Amalekites and rescued the women and children.

The Bible says that His strength is made perfect through our weakness.

"When we are weak, He is strong for us."

— 2 CORINTHIANS 12:11

This is a clear indication that the enemy of our souls is a coward. He watches and waits for our vulnerable moment and then attacks. We have to remember that at all times, God is our defense.

"The Lord shall fight for you, and ye shall hold your peace."

— EXODUS 14:14

Imagine being a leader like David, who had to experience the disappointment of his people. The enemy took everything they owned, including their families, which caused the people to be distressed. Like David, when we live a life based upon our abilities, we will fail every time. And no matter how you seek to please people, what you do or don't do will never be enough. When you aim to please someone with a carnal mindset that lacks the heart of God, it will never be enough. You may toil day and night, and it will be as if you accomplished nothing. Our best may not be good enough, but when you do it with the mindset of obedience to God, while spreading His love, it will always be pleasing to Him. And that's all that truly matters!

HEAL THE WOUND

I recently watched a movie centered around a family of four: husband, wife, daughter, and son. The family lived in a predominately high-class neighborhood. The children attended one of the top-notch schools. As parents, they tried to provide a wholesome atmosphere for their children. They wanted to make sure they had everything they needed to have a successful future. However, things still didn't turn out the way they would have liked. The son struggled with unresolved issues from the death of his biological mother. The father tried so hard to make sure that he steered him in the right direction that he failed to recognize that his son was hurting. He showed his son the discipline he needed to see, but he was unable to notice that his heart was bleeding. The effects of this manifested in his relationship, as he mistakenly murdered his girlfriend and was sentenced to life in prison. He wasn't a young boy raised in a poverty-stricken area; he didn't have a challenging upbringing. He had everything he could even think to ask for. The family also attended church on Sundays. However, the son had unresolved pain that wasn't adequately addressed.

The father gave him everything he could have ever wanted, while attempting to protect him from life's dangers. Meanwhile, the father missed how his son felt. The father was trying to be like God and make sure things didn't happen negatively to him, but didn't realize that he couldn't prevent certain things from happening.

One thing we have to realize is that the past will pass you by. Unresolved issues and unhealed hurt may ultimately pass, leaving you with pain and open wounds. Over time, your wounds may get infected and may eventually affect other areas of your life. This demonstrates our need for God. You may have everything you think you need in life, but without God's divine assistance, you won't have the strategies to conquer the things that only God has the power to change. God has blessed us with instincts and abilities to solve many complex challenges. But there are many things in our lives that we cannot fix, which takes divine intervention. We can try to correct it on our own, but we may find ourselves in cycles of disappointment, only to realize that we need God's help.

"And, behold, the Lord passed by, and a great and strong wind rent the mountains, and broke in pieces the rocks before the Lord; but the Lord was not in the wind: and after the wind an earthquake; but the Lord was not in the earthquake: And after the earthquake a fire; but the Lord was not in the fire: and after the fire a still small voice."

— 1 KINGS 19:11-12

This is an example of how we look for answers in so many things, but often, the answer is right in front of our faces. Some people may have said to themselves: "Something told me to do this" or "I felt so strongly to do that," not realizing that those little inklings or spontaneous thoughts are God's way of guiding our steps, while trying to steer us in the right direction. Some of us don't recognize when God is speaking. He can speak to us through various means, such as: scriptures, songs, movies, visions, dreams, thoughts, or people. He may even choose to speak directly to us through a still, small voice— barely above the sound of a whisper. Wherever you are, God will give you what you need, especially when you're open! And no matter how He speaks, when you hear His voice, you will feel much peace and contentment.

Within this movie, I received so much healing. God touched on many areas within me that I didn't realize were still present, but suppressed. While watching the movie, I was open. I was open and ready to receive what He had in store for me. I didn't realize that I had similar traits as the father, wanting my son to be protected from the harmful aspects of this world. I didn't want my son to feel like he had to perfect just because of how careful I was with him. So, I allowed God to flow through me, as I received healing from the shame of being pregnant out of wedlock, feeling abandoned, experiencing neglect, and being a single mom.

You may be wondering: Why did all of this happen the way that it did? God is very strategic in all that He does. He knows that we are led by our subconscious, as it runs our life. That's why He made sure that certain things are addressed at specific times. And if the timing isn't right for a particular issue to be addressed, He may put us in an induced coma, just until it's time for it to be dealt with. Just as a doctor would wait until a patient's swelling goes down before admitting them for surgery, as a result of a major injury, we, too, must sometimes wait until our mental or emotional swelling goes down before it's time for God's operation.

REFLECT/ JOURNAL

RESOURCES FOR CHAPTER FOUR

Let's take a moment to revisit some moments in time where these words reflect that moment.

What memories do you have of the following emotions?

Love
Joy
Hurt
Disappointment
Accomplished

All of these memories produced something, though we may sometimes think that some were not beneficial to our lives, especially the unpleasant ones. They were valuable lessons learned that produced much growth and maturity. Now, you can help others do the same.

If for some reason you feel as though you are not healed from any of the areas that were unpleasant, repeat this prayer below.

Father in the Name of Jesus, we present this emotion to you, and we pray for divine healing. We invite the Holy Spirit to be exercised to bring healing and perspective regarding the whole matter. Amen.

4

MIND WHAT MATTERS

The battlefield of the mind is where it all begins. When you pay close attention, you may notice that many things *were gathered* throughout your entire life. Notice I said *"were gathered,"* and not *"gathered by you,"* as some things were gathered without your knowledge. Most times, information is subconsciously collected from the situations we've encountered. Every situation has matter. Since the time of our conception, we've collected matter. Let's take a trip back to the origins of humanity.

IN THE BEGINNING

From the beginning, humanity was placed in the Garden of Eden, where they *dwelled in the presence of the Lord—* the presence of Truth.

"For you have made the Lord, my refuge, even the Most High, your dwelling place. No evil will befall you, nor will my plague come near your tent."

— PSALM 91:9-10

CRYSTAL LOVE

But they got distracted.

"You were running well; who hindered you from obeying the truth?"

— GALATIANS 5:7

The enemy had a plan. His objective was to remove humanity from the presence of God. To do that, he wanted to *persuade them to disobey God*. Disobedience is a sin that leads to death.

"For the wages of sin is death, but the gift of God is eternal life in Christ Jesus our Lord."

— ROMANS 6:23

To go forward, you must examine your past. Some may wonder, *"Why do I think this way?"* or "Why do I react this way?" Or, just simply: **WHY AM I THIS WAY?**

Memories from your past can extend back to the time in your mother's womb. Whether they were good or bad memories, they contributed towards who you are and how you think. You are what you think, and the world around you helped to determine this! That means you can pick up influences from your family, friends, and coworkers. That's why the Bible admonishes us to be careful about adhering to the ways of the world.

"Don't copy the behavior and customs of this world, but let God transform you into a new person by changing the way you think. Then you will learn to know God's will for you, which is good and pleasing and perfect."

— ROMANS 12:2

MY PREGNANCY WITH JOSHUA

The day I found out I was pregnant, I experienced the fear of the unknown, but excitement at the same time. I always wondered what pregnancy was like full-term, but fear gripped me, as I thought about my miscarriage three years prior. Though unexpected, I was looking forward to the journey. The idea of a human being growing and developing inside of my body was an amazing miracle that only God could do! One the day of my first appointment, I walked into the doctor's office, excited to see my gift from God. I heard his little heartbeat, which made me so happy inside. And although he appeared to be the size of a pea, I appreciated this early stage of his life. Human life, at its conception, is a human. I was able to order a 3D sonogram, which was so fascinating. It gave me an idea of what my little baby boy would look like, while preparing for his arrival!

Promote Life

To the man or woman who is considering terminating a human life, I ask that you reconsider! Regardless of what took place or how it took place, know that it wasn't a mistake. Nothing God created was a mistake. You may regret the timing and choices you made, but even if pregnancy occurs, you must accept responsibility for your actions despite your non-intention to conceive. You must keep in mind that everyone God created has a purpose. God will make the necessary provisions and give assurance and assistance when needed. Alternatively, adoption may be another choice. Many married couples struggle with conception and would love to adopt a baby to take care of. Therefore, we must protect the sacredness of life and ensure that we don't abort the life of a child that God created.

Single Moms

You are not in this alone. God will send you a support system. He will send you someone who will be there to stand in the gap for you spiritually and naturally, even if your child's father purposely leaves you to raise your child alone. The feeling of abandonment may be painful, but during this time, continue to press forward with focus and determination, knowing that many have survived this, and you will too!

Single moms, your children need you. And now is the time when you can begin depositing in them. You can start depositing in them before they are born.

When I was pregnant with my son, I played music with a machine on my stomach. And at eleven years old, my son loves music to this day! He has been reading music and playing the piano for over six years. He loves music so much that he hums throughout the day. As a mother, this was something that I valued as essential to impart to him. And now, I see its effects and how it has flourished in him throughout the years.

CONSIDER THE SEEDS YOU SOW

It all begins with a seed. And that seed can produce a harvest. Imagine having a garden with many planted seeds. The seeds will require watering to grow. When the seeds develop and bloom, you will be able to enjoy the beauty of your garden. But this garden isn't just for you, as others will be able to reap from its harvest. You will have more than enough to share, as relationships are give-and-take. People need what's in your garden, as you need from theirs, as well. And when you are enlightened within, it will shine on the outside. You will become attractive, and people will be drawn to your garden.

We must harvest crops for ourselves and others to survive. We must share what we have. Many need our support, but we can't do it alone. Therefore, it takes God's power to produce and quench the hunger of others in the world. So, we need supernatural watering for our gardens to produce an overflowing amount of nourishment for those who are malnourished.

This principle extends beyond the physical, as we are all spiritual beings living in this world. Because of this fact, not only do we need natural food, but we must learn to thrive on a supernatural diet. This is apparent when you consider those who have significant fame and fortune, but still aren't satisfied. They may quickly come to realize that worldly things will never fulfill our needs. We cannot enjoy the things of this world unless we have Christ on the inside. It's His presence that gives us true peace and joy.

"The earth is the Lord's, and the fullness thereof; the world, and they that dwell therein."

— PSALM 24:1

God created the earth for us to enjoy— to dress it and to keep it. While here, we are to be fruitful and multiply, as we steward the land He has given us.

"And the LORD God took the man and put him into the garden of Eden to dress it and to keep it."

— GENESIS 2:15

As God's children, are we caring for what he has entrusted us? This is our earth; this is our territory! If anything takes place on the earth that's not conducive to growth and productivity, it must go! That's why we must be aware of what's being deposited in our environment. This means that we need Godly people in leadership and governmental positions to carry God's principles in the earth. Whenever a nation is falling, we can often find a toxic seed in leadership!

TAKE RESPONSIBILITY

If you reside in a home, whether you own it, rent it, or live with someone else, it is your responsibility to pay the bills. Such bills may include the: mortgage or rent, gas and electric, and water bills. There may also be additional expenses that are necessary to stay in the home. Along with the responsibility of bills, cleaning is very important. Your home needs to be clean and comfortable for yourself and guests who may visit.

When you come home, you most likely close the door and lock it. *Why?* This is because everyone doesn't have the same concept of right and wrong. Everyone doesn't have the same convictions. We live in a world filled with many people who have not chosen Christ to be their Savior. So, they are led by the Prince of the Power of the Air, who is the enemy of our souls— Satan. And with many influences surrounding us, we can choose to do evil or good. Therefore, some people may break into your home if you leave your door unlocked. They may steal the possessions that you have worked hard for and attempt to harm you. Therefore, wisdom lets us know that it is our responsibility to guard our homes.

So, take a moment to think about God and His creation. When he created the heavens and the earth, He gave us specific instructions on what to do with everything. Although we have been given charge over the earth, God has given us specific instructions on ensuring that things run smoothly. When you think of the earth as your home, you may change your perspective on caring for it. It's time to consider what you can do to change the things going on in the earth. And this change begins with you.

When you get around family and friends, are you carnal-minded and complain about what is or isn't happening? Or, do you go in prayer and seek the Father in heaven to find out what He wants to be done on the earth? We must remember that it's not our will that matters, but it's Christ's will that shall be done on earth, as it is in heaven.

"Your kingdom come, Your will be done, on earth as it is in heaven."

— MATTHEW 6:10

Oftentimes, thoughts manifest into action. Once an action takes place, it can't be undone. For every action, there is a reaction. Some actions may have worked out in your favor, whereas others may not have turned out the way you planned. I often said to myself, "I wish I knew then what I know now! My life would have been so much further along than it is now!" But one thing I realized is that we should never live life with regret! This is one of the most dangerous things that you can do to sabotage your future. The fact remains that there is **absolutely nothing** we can do about what has already happened! We can study the past, learn from the situation, and adapt better problem-solving skills for the future. Knowing this is so liberating! We owe it to ourselves to be free from the bondage of regret. No matter the mistake or how faulted we think we are, when God sees us, He speaks differently of us.

He declares that *we are good!*

"God saw all that he had made, and it was very good. And there was evening, and there was morning the sixth day."

— GENESIS 1:31

We are *fearfully and wonderfully made!*

"I will praise You, for I am fearfully and wonderfully made; marvelous are Your works, and that my soul knows very well."

— PSALM 139:14

His love for us *covers a multitude of sins.*

"Above all, love each other deeply, because love covers over a multitude of sins."

— 1 PETER 4:8

What's in your mind determines how you respond to life's situations. What's on your mind also determines what's in your heart. This is why our ultimate prayer should be that God will give us a new mind and heart to build upon. **It's time to reset!**

REFLECT/ JOURNAL

RESOURCES FOR CHAPTER FIVE

Refer to the 30 Day Devotional
Day 7: "The Importance of Consistency"
(*Available November 2021*)

To help with planning and consistency, scan below to purchase the Visionary's Planner.

Scan below to listen to the prayer to get back on course. For access, use the password: Listen.

What are the most common distractions that come to take your attention off of your vision?

____ Television   ____ Insecurities
____ Social Media   _____ (other)
____ Phone   _____ (other)
____ Past Failures   _____ (other)

How do you overcome those distractions?

1. Write your vision.
2. Pray over your vision.
3. Plan the steps to start.

5

FOCUS FOR PRODUCTIVITY

To make progress in any area of life, it requires focus. According to the Oxford Dictionary, "focus" can be described as "the state or quality of having or producing clear visual definition." And for those who wear glasses, sometimes this requires a prescription.

WHAT CAN YOU SEE?

I was recently told by my eye doctor that I needed glasses— but only to see objects that were far away! I was told that I was nearsighted and could only see objects that were close by. I discovered that nighttime was the most challenging time for me to see. However, I noticed that I was able to drive during the day without glasses, but only if I traveled along routes that I was familiar with. Even though particular objects were far away, my knowledge of the lights and curves on the road helped me to navigate my way along the route. I was even able to drive with confidence at a higher speed! But in areas that I wasn't familiar with, I had to put on my glasses and drive at a slower pace, paying close attention to everything around me. It was during that time that I had to be extra careful of what was ahead. I had to shut down all distractions. I turned off the radio and ceased all conversations in order to concentrate on my final destination. If

I missed a turn, I would either take a detour or turn around and get on a familiar route. And usually, that happened when I didn't have on my eyeglasses. However, if I took the time to put on my glasses, I wouldn't have to worry about getting lost or arriving at my destination in a timely fashion. That's because my eyeglasses were designed to help me focus and see clearly.

GET BACK ON COURSE

So take a moment to think about the help that God has given us. He knows the plans that He has for our lives. He gives us access to pray to Him and to get detailed instructions on every route we should take in life. But what if we've made a significant detour; *how do we get back on course?*

Prayer To Get Back On Course

My Beloved Father, in the Name of Jesus, we pray for extra x-ray vision, as we are looking to pursue our destiny. We know that you desire for us to make it to every place that You have predestined for us to encounter. So, we turn on our navigation, which is the Holy Spirit. And we declare in the Name of Jesus that though we may not know exactly where we're going, that we will be wholly dependent upon You. You are our navigation system and will help us arrive at every preordained destination on time!

In the Name of Jesus, Amen.

Some of us have to acknowledge that we need glasses. I am forty years old and did not need glasses up until now. But, I noticed that as I've gotten older, things that came naturally are no longer as effortless. Therefore, I have to concentrate more and work harder to get things done. This may be a result of frustration, being worn down, or simply the aging process. And although aging is a natural process, there are many things that we can do to remain healthy in our mind, body, and spirit.

Consider implementing the following:

1. Develop spiritual strength.

Our entire focus must be on Jesus. We can do this by incorporating the fundamentals of praying, fasting, studying the Bible, worshipping, and fellowshipping with other Believers.

Key Verses to Remember:

- "Do not be anxious about anything, but in every situation, by prayer and petition, with thanksgiving, present your requests to God. And the peace of God, which transcends all understanding, will guard your hearts and your minds in Christ Jesus." — *Philippians 4:6-7*

- "So we fasted and petitioned our God about this, and he answered our prayer." — *Ezra 8:23*

- "When the peoples are gathered together, And the kingdoms, to serve the LORD." — *Psalm 102:22*

- "All Scripture is breathed out by God and profitable for teaching, for reproof, for correction, and training in righteousness, that the man of God may be competent, equipped for every good work." — *2 Timothy 3:16-17*

2. Practice spiritual discipline.

Make daily time with God through prayer and meditation. Be intentional about planning time to spend with God. Consider spending time with Him in the morning before starting your day. Establish a daily devotional routine and time for studying the Bible. You can implement this during your lunch break or even at night before bed. Time with our Heavenly Father is time well spent. One hour with God can give you instructions for the next ten years of your life. He knows the blueprint of our lives, and if we ask, He will share everything in its time. Whether it's through Him directly or through other avenues, He will ensure that we receive the information we need to know.

Key Verses to Remember:

- "A person without self-control is like a city with broken-down walls." — *Proverbs 25:28*

- "To everything, there is a season and a time to every purpose under the heaven." — *Ecclesiastes 3:1*

- "But he answered and said, It is written, Man shall not live by bread alone, but by every word that proceedeth out of the mouth of God." — *Matthew 4:4*

- "For I know the thoughts that I think toward you, saith the Lord, thoughts of peace, and not of evil, to give you an expected end. Then shall ye call upon me, and ye shall go and pray unto me, and I will hearken unto you. And ye shall seek me and find me when ye shall search for me with all your heart." — *Jeremiah 29:11-13*

3. Pray for an accountability partner.

Having an accountability partner can help ensure that you complete each of your assigned tasks in a timely fashion. There may be seasons in our lives where we may be motivated and productive. There may be other times when we could benefit from someone checking in on us and encouraging us to remain focused. Your accountability partner shouldn't someone that you rely heavily upon, but rather, someone that will commit to supporting you throughout the time that was established.

Key Verses to Remember:

- "Trust in the Lord with all your heart, and do not lean on your own understanding. In all your ways acknowledge Him, and He will make straight your paths." — *Proverbs 3:5-6*

- "It is better to take refuge in the Lord than to trust in man." — *Psalm 118:8*

4. Strive for effective production.

Don't just strive to produce, but your goal should be to produce effectively. Each of us has an individual uniqueness and greatness that God has imparted into all of us as human beings. We truly have so much to offer to the world. And although we can learn a skill and master it, that doesn't necessarily mean that it's part of your purpose here on earth. It merely means that you can do what you discipline yourself to master. You may have begun something and achieved a high state of productivity while doing it, but it doesn't necessarily mean that that's what you're supposed to be producing in life.

I am an entrepreneur and a visionary. God has given me the ability to take something and make a product of it. God has shown me that we have to focus on one thing at a time. And before we commit our time and talents to start a new project, we must make sure that it's what we are supposed to be doing. Just because I have the money, it doesn't mean that I should start a manufacturing business. Regardless of its ability to produce significant wealth, it doesn't mean that it connects to God's purpose for my life. We must understand that all of God's creation is good, and is designed to flourish. However, we must be careful to thrive within the confines of our purpose.

Key Verses to Remember:

- "God blessed them and said to them, "Be fruitful and increase in number; fill the earth and subdue it." — *Genesis 1:28*

- "I will give you every place where you set your foot, as I promised Moses." — *Joshua 1:3*

- "For the LORD God is our sun and our shield. He gives us grace and glory. The LORD will withhold no good thing from those who do what is right." — *Psalms 84:11*

- "Through our union with Christ, we too have been claimed by God as his own inheritance. Before we were even born, he gave us our destiny; that we would fulfill the plan of God who always accomplishes every purpose and plan in his heart." — *Ephesians 1:11*

- "We are reborn into a perfect inheritance that can never perish, never be defiled, and never diminish. It is promised and preserved forever in the heavenly realm for you!" — *1 Peter 1:4*

All of the promises spoken by God over our lives are sure. I have seen many things happen as a result of speaking His Word over a situation. Praying God's Word brings results!

REFLECT/ JOURNAL

RESOURCES FOR CHAPTER SIX

Refer to the 30 Day Devotional
Day 18: "Don't Miss The Moment"
(*Available November 2021*)

Take a moment to think about setting your alarm clock. You set it for a particular time, and because of the tiredness of your body, you either, sleep through it or hit the snooze button.

Have you ever felt as if you hit the snooze button of your dreams too many times and that you'd be further along in your life if you would've woke up after hearing the first alarm?

Many of us in life may feel this way. But today, let's reset the alarm. Wake up and be present at every moment and every opportunity to shine through to bring the light of God to the world, by fulfilling your purpose. God has it all under control and will redeem the time you lost when you overslept and decided to stay where you were. Make the decision, today, not to miss the moment to shine. Don't miss the moment to show up. Don't miss the moment to be You! The world needs 'you' to create change and bring resolution to the issues in the world.

RESOURCES FOR CHAPTER SIX

Pretend as if the following are alarms for moments that you want to set in your life to show up on time. Some examples are provided in the parathesis.
Now, set your own alarms.

6am-8am (ex: go back to school) _____

12pm-2pm (ex: get married) _____

3pm-5pm (ex: go to counseling) _____

6pm-8pm _____

9pm-11pm _____

12am _____

6

BE SHOCKED

Transitioning from what's comfortable to something new can be life-changing. When I was twelve years old, my family and I moved to North Carolina. I was initially shocked by the idea of moving to another state with my dad and two brothers, but eventually, I became comfortable. When my dad first mentioned this move was for ministry purposes, it was a big shock. But at the same time, because he was our father and protector, I felt confident about his decision. So I trusted him and went along for the journey.

WELCOME TO NORTH CAROLINA

Leaving Baltimore City was a big deal. I experienced a major culture shock when we arrived in North Carolina. My family and I arrived at a place that was completely different from our normal. Although it was different, I looked at it as a fresh start.

I was scheduled to start summer school in Baltimore that summer, but things changed when I moved to North Carolina. To graduate and go to the ninth grade, I was told that I had to attend summer school. I had to do this because I missed too many days of school during the school year. So, I thought that I would have to repeat the eighth grade once I moved to

North Carolina since that was the original plan if I stayed in Baltimore. However, God made it so that I didn't have to! My new school in North Carolina didn't question anything about summer school or how my eighth grade year in Baltimore went. My transcripts were received, and I was approved to start the ninth grade. Needless to say, I was extremely happy.

Although moving to North Carolina was a major transition, I had lots of family who lived down there, which ultimately softened the blow. And things weren't as bad because they were familiar with the city, and showed me all around. I remember going to football practices, basketball games, and football games— along with going to the mall and the bowling alley! Our weekends were so much fun! My dad was our driver, and he allowed us to have our freedom! Those were the good old days, back when things were simple. And just to think, I used to be in a hurry to grow up fast, before knowing all of what adulthood entailed. Responsibility, accountability, and decision-making were not on my mind at the time. But this was my journey, and it was well worth the wait — the good, bad, and indifferent. It was all part of my normal, although, at the time, my teenage mindset was set on having a good time with my cousins!

Living with my cousins made things so much easier for me. They were not only my family, but my friends at school. Having them around made it so much easier for me to adapt to school, but at the same time, it wasn't that easy, because I was still shy. Most of my life, I was timid. As a child, my timidity was often mistaken as meanness because I was quiet and stayed to myself most of the time. The only time I spoke was when I was comfortable with someone that I knew. And when a new person got to know me, they realized that I was a nice person. Being misunderstood was not my fault. But after going to school and dealing with my peers and their personalities, it was hard for me to understand why they couldn't accept my difference and quiet demeanor. They expected me to be more outspoken because I was from Baltimore City— a horrible stereotype that didn't apply to me.

Unfortunately, Baltimore City had a bad reputation for being poverty-stricken, having a high crime rate, and being a fast-paced society. These stereotypes have negatively characterized Baltimore because of what is promoted on social media, the news, and through hearsay. Some parts of the city are lovely, but most of the time, what gets projected is the negativity. And this is a prime example of how the evil in this world is more acknowledged than the good. This is why those of us that carry the Good News— the *Gospel of Jesus Christ*— need to lift our voices to proclaim the Gospel and promote positivity. There are so many great things to discuss about God's creation and good deeds to celebrate.

"For I am not ashamed of the gospel of Christ: for it is the power of God unto salvation to every one that believeth; to the Jew first, and also to the Greek."

— ROMANS 1:16

DO YOU FIT?

Fights, jealousy, and misunderstandings— you name it— I went through it in this major transition. Coming from a big city— even though people in Baltimore say it's a small world— it was an even smaller world in the little town of North Carolina that we stayed in. And although there were many good moments and great experiences, I often found myself coming home from school sad and depressed. I wanted to move back to Baltimore with my friends and family because I didn't feel like my peers accepted me. I was labeled as a city girl, and people mainly picked on me because I was quiet. But after a couple of years, I got used to the culture and the new pace of living. I also developed new friendships, which made living in that new town more pleasurable.

When you transition from one culture to another or have to adapt to someone else's culture, it can be quite uncomfortable. It requires you to understand that wherever you go, people may not resemble what you're used to, and the atmosphere may not always function the same. There may be a difference in how things take place and how they are perceived. Things may not look like what you're used to because you are in a new place. Because of that, some people feel like they don't fit in— no matter where they go! But some people are for you! These are the people who may be in your inner circle and allow you to feel comfortable being yourself. There is a vast world full of people that you haven't yet met; there are plenty of opportunities to befriend others! And although we are not meant to be close to everyone, according to the Bible, we are to love everyone. The Word of God declares that we are to love our neighbor as ourselves. That does not mean that we have to be friends with everyone that we meet. It means that we have to do right and show love at all times. This includes having a heart of forgiveness.

"Master, which is the great commandment in the law? Jesus said unto him, Thou shalt love the Lord thy God with all thy heart, and with all thy soul, and with all thy mind. This is the first and great commandment. And the second is like unto it, Thou shalt love thy neighbor as thyself."

— MATTHEW 22:36-39

Scripture informs us that the first commandment is to love God with all of your heart, and the second is to love others as yourself. This reveals to us that God desires to be the number one priority and that everything else should follow. When we love God first, we are positioned to love family, friends, and others that we meet. Like looking in the mirror and telling yourself, "Hey, I love you," we should be able to share that same love with others. If you aren't able to look in the mirror and say "I love you" to yourself, it may be hard to give love to someone else effectively. The only way that we can truly love someone else is if we receive the love of God first. It's His love that we share with others. So until we receive His love, we won't be able to love ourselves or share His love with others. It's hard to give something that we don't have ourselves. Therefore, God teaches us how to love through the example of His love for us. He teaches us by loving us unconditionally.

Despite the things that we do, He continues to love us. And although there may be consequences for our actions, it does not stop His love from flowing to us. We must continue to model the same type of love with others. We must be willing to forgive and to love others unconditionally.

> Be kind and compassionate to one another, forgiving each other, just as in Christ God forgave you.
>
> — EPHESIANS 4:32

LIVING SPIRITUALLY IN THE FLESH

Whether we want to admit it or not, we are spirit beings. Our Father in Heaven is a spirit being and the Creator of all life. Let's examine the story of Jesus. He was both human and spirit. And through Jesus, God showed us exactly how we are to function in the earth. Jesus was simply put here to save the world. His purpose was to die for our sins so that we can be redeemed back to our Father in Heaven. And just like Jesus, we are here for a reason. Each of us has an assignment here on earth.

When we separated from our Father in Heaven, we were born into the earthly realm through a woman— our mother. When we entered into the world, we were born into sin and shaped in iniquity. And although we are flesh, our spirit man yearns reconnection with our Father in Heaven. When someone comes along and introduces us to the Good News of Jesus Christ, we are then saved and reconnected with our Heavenly Father. At that moment, there is a sense of peace and contentment because that is exactly where we are supposed to be.

Anyone who experiences the presence of God can attest to the fact that such an experience cannot adequately be described. It compares to nothing you've ever experienced before. And similarly, being in a culture where we are forced to live as human beings when we are spiritual beings, can be quite uncomfortable. After acknowledging who we are and how we arrived, it's hard to continue living in a foreign land and adapt to a humanistic culture.

CULTURE SHOCK

A culture shock is an experience that may take place when you move from one cultural environment to another that is different from yours. It may manifest itself through the disorientation you may feel when experiencing an unfamiliar way of life. This feeling may arise due to the effects of visiting a new country, moving between social environments, or transitioning to another style of life.

When you desire to walk into a new way of life, things may look different. Various customs and traditions that were passed throughout your family may not be apparent in this new environment. Similarly, when you become a Christian, this new life is not the same.

When you walk in the freedom of God, you may experience a culture shock that may cause you to be reluctant to accept this new way of living. But God wants us to live free from culture shock, as this type of shock may cause fear! Fear is a torment that causes you to search for relief from someone or something. However, when we are able to change our perspectives, we are more likely to smoothly transition from one place to the next, one lifestyle to another, and one mindset to another. Change is good, even if it was sudden. Sometimes, it may feel as if we were forced into a change, in order to receive immediate breakthrough from where we are. Other times, we may have been able to gracefully walk into a change with contentment in our hearts, accepting that a transition was needed. But however our change takes place, whether conditions are favorable or not, it's important to understand the need for adjustment.

IT'S TIME FOR CHANGE

Think about how you were raised in your household. You may have been accustomed to certain traditions. A tradition in my family was going to church. We attended church every Sunday morning and during the week for Bible class. This was a common, weekly practice for our family. My grandmother was the pastor, and my mom was the children's Sunday school teacher. In addition, my mom served as a choir member and an usher. My dad sang in the choir and served as a preacher and prophet. Attending church was fun and exciting. I loved the music and enjoyed watching people praise God. I always wanted to know what people were feeling to make them react the way that they did. I was always curious as a little girl. I heard all of the Bible stories, and I knew that God was real, but I wanted to have my own personal experience. As a young teenager, I didn't understand the importance of being saved and living the life that God planned for us to live. I just knew that salvation was the right thing to do because it was all that I knew from birth. Outside of my home and church was an entirely different world. I had to adjust to what I knew, while still longing to fit in with others around me that may not have had the same upbringing. This can be very difficult to adjust to. Wanting to fit in with people who may live by unethical standards may be challenging. It requires you to be strong so that you can stand your ground against being lured into unethical standards of living, for the gratification of acceptance.

As I grew of age and experience, I realized that I can be in a different environment and still maintain who I am. A culture shock has the potential to throw you off from reality— your *normal* reality. One of the benefits of going outside of your culture is that it gives you the ability to be more openminded and understanding of those around you. You don't have to conform to the way that they do things, but you can learn to be comfortable in who you are and never forget your foundation.

Just because it's your foundation, it doesn't necessarily mean that it's morally right or Biblically sound. Family traditions and religious customs take place all the time and are passed on, regardless of its validity. But when you begin to understand more of who you are and what God created you to be, you are better equipped to see things clearly. You will then be able to weed out some of the things that you once viewed as a rule of thumb and realize that at any moment if you discontinued it, it can't define you. The only thing we stand sure of and firm on, regardless of human opinion, is the Biblical principles in the Word of God.

"Heaven and earth shall pass away, but my words will never pass away."

— MATTHEW 24:35

TRUST & OBEY

As a frame of reference, we can reflect on the story of Abram, whose name was changed by God to Abraham. Abraham was told that he would be the father of many nations, but that he had to leave his country.

"Now the Lord had said unto Abram, 'Get thee out of thy country, and from thy kindred, and from thy father's house, unto a land that I will shew thee: And I will make of thee a great nation, and I will bless thee, and make thy name great, and thou shalt be a blessing; And I will bless them that bless thee, and use him that curseth thee: and in thee shall all families of the earth be blessed.' So Abram departed, as the Lord had spoken to him; and Lot went with him; and Abram was seventy and five years old when he departed out of Haran."

— GENESIS 12:1-4

Before Abraham was able to become a father of many nations, one thing, in particular, had to happen— he had to leave his home and travel to a foreign country. This transition was very significant to the plan God had for Abraham's life.

"And the days of Terah were two hundred and five years, and Terah died in Haran."

— GENESIS 11:32

Scripture reveals to us that Abraham's father, Terah, died in the land of Haran. Although he was en route to Canaan— the Promised Land— he was not who God chose to lead and be the father of many nations. God chose Abraham and told him to get out of his country, away from his family and his father's house. God was taking him to a new land that only He could show him. These instructions were given to Abraham after the death of his father. One of the mistakes that Abraham made was taking his nephew Lot with him. God was clear when He instructed him to leave his family and his father's house. Because he chose to take his nephew, many complications took place. *Two visions with two leaders will clash if God has not given instructions for there to be a collaboration.* And because of that, Abraham and Lot eventually split up due to there being confusion. Learning to obey God fully serves as a great foundational blueprint. From Abraham's mistake, we can understand the importance of obedience, while being aware that God's grace allows us to recover after we've made decisions that have caused detours in our lives.

When God told Abraham to leave, he was told to leave everything familiar. This included his country, his family, and his father's home. God wanted him to change his whole atmosphere and go to a new environment. I'm pretty certain that this probably served as an initial shock to Abraham. But at the same time, he trusted the voice of the Lord and knew that He would not steer him in the wrong direction. Abraham understood that God created him; he accepted that He knows what's best and what's ahead.

In addition, Jesus' life was the perfect example of trust and obedience. He was birthed into the world through the supernatural conception of the Holy Spirit. Mary, I'm sure, was humbled and honored to birth the Savior of the world into the earth. Jesus, who is God in the flesh, came into the world as a baby and grew into a man who restored the relationship of man back to God, our Father.

Even as a child, Jesus knew his purpose. And although He had physical parents, He didn't allow them to get in the way of His divine assignment on earth. Luke captures the account of Jesus staying behind in Jerusalem, as it was an annual custom for his parents to celebrate the Festival of the Passover.

"Every year, Jesus' parents went to Jerusalem for the Festival of the Passover. When he was twelve years old, they went up to the festival, according to the custom. After the festival was over, while his parents were returning home, the boy Jesus stayed behind in Jerusalem, but they were unaware of it. After three days they found him in the temple courts, sitting among the teachers, listening to them and asking them questions. Everyone who heard him was amazed at his understanding and his answers. When his parents saw him, they were astonished. His mother said to him, "Son, why have you treated us like this? Your father and I have been anxiously searching for you."

— LUKE 2:41-48

At the age of twelve, Jesus understood the importance of ministry. He did not allow anything to stand in His way. His age not only reminds us of His divine focus as a child, as Hebrew boys become men at the age of thirteen, but it also symbolizes governmental authority in correlation to the twelve tribes of Israel. But after three days of his parents searching for Him, His response revealed to them the true intent of His heart— His deep passion for the things of God!

It's notable to consider the effectiveness of both translations.

"Why were you searching for me?" he asked. "Didn't you know I had to be in my Father's house?"

— LUKE 2:49 NIV

"And He said to them, "Why did you seek Me? Did you not know that I must be about My Father's business?"

— LUKE 2:49 NKJV

At the age of thirty, Jesus began His ministry.

"Coming to his hometown, he began teaching the people in their synagogue, and they were amazed. 'Where did this man get this wisdom and these miraculous powers?' they asked. 'Isn't this the carpenter's son? Isn't his mother's name Mary, and aren't his brothers James, Joseph, Simon, and Judas. Aren't all his sisters with us? Where then did this man get all these things?' And they took offense at him. But Jesus said to them, 'A prophet is not without honor except in his own town and in his own home.'"

— MATTHEW 13:54-57

In life, we must understand that there will be a time where we must leave people, cultures, and traditions. Then, we can cleave to new, adventurous, God-centered paths! When we adhere to our predestined paths, we can truly break free from the past. *Do you want to be free and stay free?! Do you want to live a life that you didn't think was possible?* Well, today is your day! Pray, and God will guide your next steps.

You may be thinking, "But how do I know what He's saying," as you may have struggled with understanding the voice of God. Some people express this sentiment by saying, "Something told me" or "I just have this feeling in my gut." Some may even express that they happen to feel strongly to move in a certain direction, without the understanding as to why. A lot of us are led by God and don't even know we are. *How can this be?* This is because we are spiritual beings. God created us with intellect, ideas, and vision. They have been deposited in us and throughout our lives. He gives us glimpses of His will for our lives. Therefore, we may feel certain urges to move in a certain direction or to react in a certain way. And sometimes, we don't always move on those instincts. Furthermore, not everyone may be God-conscious. You may know that He exists, but you may not have a full understanding of how everything operates, as it pertains to the world that we live in.

Many of us have questioned God about creation. *How did we get here? Why are we here? Why do certain things happen in the world...if there is a God?* Our Father in Heaven, the Creator of all things, can answer all of our questions. When we are in a relationship with Him, God can help us find answers to the questions we have in our hearts. It is through the Word of God, prayer, and others in the body of Christ that we can receive those answers and attain resolve for every question and concern. And because we can trust God with our lives, especially when He's told us to move in a certain direction, we should not be afraid or fearful of what's ahead. We can move forward, knowing that we will make it through any circumstance that may arise because we have an expected end. This is how we must live life as Believers, knowing that we can trust God's promises. As long as you follow His instructions and stay in His perfect will for your life, you're going to win every battle. The battle is already won. Jesus accomplished all of that on the Cross when He died for our sins. So all we have to do is fight the battle that's inside of us. And to be honest with you, that's the hardest battle to fight. We must remember that it's only a fight when we haven't fully surrendered to God. There will always be a struggle between spirit and flesh when we aren't fully surrendered because your flesh will try to pull you towards the things of the world, while your spirit yearns for the things of God.

> "For I delight in the law of God after the inward man: But I see another law in my members, warring against the law of my mind, and bringing me into captivity to the law of sin which is in my members. O wretched man that I am! Who shall deliver me from the body of this death?"
>
> — ROMANS 7:22-25

I thank God for saving us through Jesus Christ, our Lord! Because of Him, we can freely serve the law of God, despite our flesh wanting to serve the law of sin. Through Scripture, the flesh is defined as that part of us that is alienated from God. The Bible refers to our spirit as the part of us that desires to commune with God. To make this clearer, think back to the cartoons you may have watched as a kid. There were cartoons that had the devil on one side of the cartoon's shoulder and an angel on the other side. As silly as this seems, that's exactly how this war looks. There is a constant battle between good and evil in the world that we live in. This war also takes place inside of us. That's why it's a blessing that God gives us parents, guardians, and other role models to help steer us down the right path. Having Godly role models can help us develop healthy morals that can serve as a foundation for us to build upon as we mature. Without a healthy foundation, it's easy to live life recklessly because there's nothing to counter the evil that seeks to overtake you. The only way you can overtake evil is with good.

> "Be not overcome of evil but overcome evil with good."
>
> — ROMANS 12:21

But to do this, we need divine assistance. We need the Spirit of God to intervene on the inside of us and to help us to stop sabotaging our lives.

That's why it makes sense to trust God with your life because He's the only One that can move us in the right direction. He helps us make the right decisions at the right time, and arrive at the right place to accomplish everything we were destined to do.

REFLECT/ JOURNAL

RESOURCES FOR CHAPTER SEVEN

Refer to the 30 Day Devotional
Day 22: "Identity Crisis"
(*Available November 2021*)

Do you know who you are? What are you made of?

We can identify with many things in life, but the most important area is identifying who you are.

Name four good qualities that you and others may have identified you with:

1. _____
2. _____
3. _____
4. _____

Name four flaws that you and others may have identified you with:

1. _____
2. _____
3. _____
4. _____

RESOURCES FOR CHAPTER SEVEN

Did you know that even in the midst of the good qualities and flaws that they measure up to the person that God said that you are?

Outside of what you do or don't do, you are these things below:

1. I am loved.

"And I am convinced that nothing can ever separate us from God's love. Neither death nor life, neither angels nor demons, neither our fears for today nor our worries about tomorrow—not even the powers of hell can separate us from God's love. No power in the sky above or in the earth below—indeed, nothing in all creation will ever be able to separate us from the love of God that is revealed in Christ Jesus our Lord" (Romans 8:38-39).

"But he was pierced for our transgressions, he was crushed for our iniquities; the punishment that brought us peace was on him, and by his wounds we are healed" (Isaiah 53:5).

RESOURCES FOR CHAPTER SEVEN

2. I am strong.

"God arms me with strength, and he makes my way perfect" (Psalm 18:32).

3. I am forgiven.

"I am writing to you who are God's children because your sins have been forgiven through Jesus" (1 John 2:12).

4. I am adopted.
"God decided in advance to adopt us into his own family by bringing us to himself through Jesus Christ. This is what he wanted to do, and it gave him great pleasure" (Ephesians 1:5).

5. I am whole.
"So you also are complete through your union with Christ, who is the head over every ruler and authority" (Colossians 2:10).

6. I am His.
"Do not fear. I have redeemed you. I have summoned you. You are mine" (Isaiah 43:1).

RESOURCES FOR CHAPTER SEVEN

7. I am accompanied.

"...Do not be afraid or discouraged. For the Lord your God is with you wherever you go" (Joshua 1:9).

Accept it by faith and allow God to heal the broken places, so that all of who He encompassed you to be can be materialized.

7

BEND TO BLEND

You have to compromise on some level to blend into the crowd. But were we made to blend? Were we made to be like everyone else? Are we supposed to do things exactly like we've seen them done before? Twins that are labeled identical have very distinct differences. God made no two individuals alike! We may have some things in common that help us connect with others, but despite such, we will always move and think differently than others. Therefore, we should never compromise our uniqueness to fit in! Most times, when you try to do this, you may stand out like a sore thumb and never truly be comfortable being someone that you were never created to be. There is much peace and contentment when you operate as God desires. The peace you experience will never rest on you; it will be continual. *But what if you're doing something that makes you prosperous?* Regardless of how wealthy you become, it will never be enough! God created us with the innate ability to learn and to master whatever we set our minds to. Just because we attend school, obtain a degree, and become proficient in a trade, that doesn't necessarily mean that we're supposed to do it. It may simply be a job, or a means for making money, but not your calling.

"I praise you because I am fearfully and wonderfully made; your works are wonderful, I know that full well."

— PSALM 139:14

DON'T COMPROMISE TO FIT IN

In High school, I feel that I compromised the most. I grew up in a home with Christian values, and I knew right from wrong. However, I didn't always make decisions based on what was imparted by my parents and other Christian leaders. When I was around certain people, I compromised my values.

One day, with friends, I planned on going inside a store to steal. I knew that this was not right, based on the standards my parents taught me and those of great influence. However, I did it anyway! What I stole was pretty inexpensive. But to me, I got a kick out of getting away with it and saving one dollar! *If I got caught, would it have been worth it? What if my reputation was tarnished over stealing an eyeliner pencil?* This was something I could have easily paid for. As a result, I experienced the adverse effects of my actions. There was a hefty price to pay for an unethical action that only took a few minutes of my time to complete. After that day, I experienced paranoia, as a direct effect of stealing that one item. I was utterly overwhelmed and realized that stealing was not the path I wanted to continue down. At that moment, I began to understand the importance of thinking before reacting and evaluating every action's consequences before making a decision.

But at a young age, you may not always know the implications of the decisions you make. You may think you know, but you don't really know what you're getting yourself into, sometimes. The choices you make can either steer you in the right or wrong direction, if you're not careful. The foundation of anything has to be secure for that building to stand. And even though I may have made decisions based on the people around me, the foundation that my parents gave me is priceless. I would not be where I am today if my parents didn't raise me the way they did.

So now, I feel a moral responsibility to help other children, teenagers, young adults, and even older adults that haven't found their way— my love is not limited to age. In addition to rearing my son in the ways of God, I have a strong desire to impart wisdom to the younger generation, as I understand what they may be going through.

Back then, I remember feeling like I was being punished because I wasn't always able to do what everyone else was doing. This doesn't take away from the beautiful memories I enjoyed, but it shows the limited perspective I had. I didn't realize that I was able to have fun, but with limits. And this principle can be applied to those in any stage of life. You have to set boundaries for how far you will go. Boundaries help to protect us. However, we must not put a boundary on God. We should never limit His access to our hearts. He is the only person that should have full reign in every area of our lives. You will notice that you have true peace and contentment when God is involved in every area of your life— even the places of pain.

I used to entertain the hurtful feelings associated with not being accepted by everyone. I would ask myself: *What is wrong with me? Am I enough?* I was timid and not outgoing. But when someone approached me to have a conversation, I would finally open up and let my guard down. I thought of myself as uninteresting, so I pretended to be someone I was not so that I could blend in. But that didn't work. I wasn't meant to blend. I was meant to **STAND OUT**.

YOU ARE ENOUGH

Many of us spend a lifetime changing who we are to be accepted and to feel good about ourselves on the inside. We may change our hair, clothes, religious statues, or even social groups to satisfy that need. But we must understand that it's crucial to accept ourselves the way we were created and see ourselves spiritually through God's lens. Whether or not someone validates us through compliments, accolades, or standing ovations, it will never be enough. You will just need more and more to fill the empty hole in your soul that only God can fill and satisfy. The praise we receive from others should never be the gauge of our thermometers. There should be an inner temperature that remains constant, so that no matter what is said or done, you will never lose sight of who you are. Regardless of our background, level of confidence, or even age— we must learn not to accept who we are based upon what others think of us or how they feel about us.

Blending takes so much energy to do. It's a lot easier and completely natural just to be yourself. Whether accepted or not, people have to accept what you present to them. Yes, we should be mindful of how others view us, but we can't change who we are because of it unless it goes against what God created you to be. What's important to you may not be important to others, but that shouldn't change things. We have to be sensitive to how others view the world, but at the same time, not compromise who we are and conform.

REFLECT/ JOURNAL

RESOURCES FOR CHAPTER EIGHT

Refer to the 30 Day Devotional
Day 23: "Understanding the Season"
Day 6: "Expectations in Perspective"
(*Available November 2021*)

Have you ever took a moment to think about what your future and your present would look like if your perspective was changed? Your perspective on life changes from your mindset. Your mindset is renewed by God's Word. Transformation in our lives comes from a changed mind.

"Stop imitating the ideals and opinions of the culture around you, but be inwardly transformed by the Holy Spirit through a total reformation of how you think. This will empower you to discern God's will as you live a beautiful life, satisfying and perfect in his eyes." -Romans 12:2

What are you expecting?

1. _____
2. _____
3. _____
4. _____

RESOURCES FOR CHAPTER EIGHT

Take a moment to stop and pray about your expectations, making sure that these are the things that God wants in your life. If it is, then it will surely happen.

Even if you're unsure about your expectations, pray and ask the Lord to give you details as to how your life and thoughts can come in alignment with His will. That way, it can happen in God's timing or be revealed to you that it shouldn't happen at all.

8

SET YOUR THERMOMETER

As a cosmetologist by trade, I've been in the beauty industry for over twenty years. It's been such a fantastic journey. I've developed some lifelong relationships that I will cherish for the rest of my life. This field of work has contributed to the woman I am today. I went from a shy, young girl who would barely talk or go anywhere alone, to an outgoing woman that can engage in conversations on my own. God knows what He's doing when He places us in different environments. I didn't realize that the beauty salon chair would also be my counseling chair!

Eight years after doing hair full-time, I started seminary school. I truly love the Word of God, and I wanted to learn more about Him, myself, and the mysteries I haven't seen. There are stories of victory, defeat, mistakes, regret, forgiveness, rebellion, overcoming fear, and others recorded within the Bible. But don't take my word for it! Read it for yourself! The Bible is an excellent read, just as your story matters, as well.

Although the Bible isn't being rewritten, please note that your story will have a lasting impression on someone else's life, many years down the line— long after you're gone. Someone will read and envision what you've been going through and how you persevered. They can learn from your story. As such, we are all students. We will forever be a student, learning from the Word of God and others that He uses to help teach us. There will never be a time where it's not a teachable moment. You can walk away from every experience, taking away something that will help you along the rest of your journey.

Needless to say, my seminary school was an enjoyable experience for me. I learned so much about myself and how to help others. At seminary, I embraced becoming a counselor. Although I originally went to seminary school to learn more about the Bible, a part of my curriculum involved taking a counseling course. This allowed me to learn more about myself and deal with the deep wounds that I ran from for years. I would have never thought that this would be the setup for something that would carry on for years. Before schooling, I informally counseled people through the guidance of the Holy Spirit. I relied on God's wisdom to accomplish His work done on the earth. And for me, that began in the beauty salon chair.

WELCOME TO HAIR CHEMISTRY

In 2017, Hair Chemistry LLC was launched. When I stepped out on faith and decided to start my business, it was out of my comfort zone, but my husband reassured me that I have what it takes to be an independent stylist. God has used him to cover and love me as a husband should.

At that time, I leased a suite through Salon Suites. It was a big building that had several suites available for independent business owners to run their salons. I ran my business there for two years. Before that, I worked in two salons, but this was my first time on my own. And it felt great!

In the salon, there was a central thermometer that set the temperature for everyone's suite. This thermometer happened to be a few feet from my suite. And for those of you who haven't experienced the side effects of being in a hair salon, it can get pretty warm rather quickly. With the presence of curler ovens, flat irons, hairdryers, and people, it got pretty toasty! And because some suites were small, it concealed even more heat. So to combat the heat, I often set the gauge on the thermometer to suit my clients and me. Oftentimes, this brought conflict, as other leasing tenants were not comfortable with the temperature that I set. Therefore, individual thermometers for every suite would have been sufficient and convenient for everyone.

WHERE IS YOUR SETTING?

This same principle is what we should practice in our lives. No one but God should set our gauge. We should never allow someone else to control our temperature. But when we allow God to set our temperature, things will be consistent. We will have a steady flow that will keep us at a comfortable temperature all-year-round. Only God knows what we need, and His Hand on the temperature gauge will ensure that our settings remain constant, despite the weather conditions around us.

Are you content with the way things are going right now in your life? Do you think it could be better? You have the ability to make a change. What temperature does your gauge read right now? Are you *hot*— as in ON FIRE — leaving a trail blaze, where others behind you will want to follow you? Or, are you barely doing the minimum?

GET UNCOMFORTABLE

Take a moment to think about where you currently are and what you could be doing to go above and beyond what's "comfortable." Once you've given it some thought, grab a journal and consider making a plan. Follow the steps below to get started with fulfilling God's plan for your life.

Steps to Fulfill God's Plan

1. Pray!

> Before you begin anything, always start with prayer. Ask God to reveal His will for your life. His wisdom will guide you in the direction you should go.

2. Write your vision.

Gather your writing utensils or a computer (or any other electronic device) to document your vision. This will serve as a formal document of God's purpose for you on the earth. Keep in mind that this may be one of the many assignments God has for you to fulfill. Having this vision statement written out is key, as it will help you stay on track when opportunities arise to take you off course. At that moment, you can go to God in prayer and say, *"It is written..."* and it shall be, as this is God's divine plan for your life.

"If you have a willing heart to let me help you, and if you will obey me, you will feast on the blessings of an abundant harvest."

— ISAIAH 1:19

---

3. Write out your goals.

Consider developing three short-term goals that support the vision God has revealed to you. Next, reflect on the things you've already done that are in line with those goals. Brainstorm a list of other actions you can take to accomplish these goals.

4. Develop a team.

With prayer, form a team of like-minded individuals who have your best interest at heart. In God's timing, He will lead you to those who have the background and heart for your vision.

5. Conduct research.

Spend some time researching the assignment you are trying to accomplish. Become familiar with the topic and learn as much as you can about it!

6. Prepare.

Consider all of the resources you may need to accomplish your goals. Write down every resource that may be relevant to your assignment.

7. Set a realistic plan.

Devise a timeline with realistic dates for specific tasks to be accomplished. Have a realistic goal in mind while you're in the planning process.

Fulfilling God's plans takes proper planning and discipline to start, maintain, and finish. In doing so, having the right mindset, proper attitude, and diligence to finish strong will be essential to your growth in every area of your life!

REFLECT/ JOURNAL

RESOURCES FOR CHAPTER NINE

Refer to the Strategies of Finding Normal
Section: "Addictions"

Refer to the 30 Day Devotional
Day 29: "Open My Eyes"
(*Available November 2021*)

Scan below to listen to the
prayer to break addictions.

For access, use the
password: Listen.

9

WALK IN MINISTRY

What is ministry? This may be a foreign word to some who may not have heard of it. And sometimes, it may be dismissed if it doesn't seem like it applies. But regardless of who you are, we all were created for ministry. So whether you have heard about this your entire life or if you are just hearing about this now— this is your time to begin! It's time to begin what God has already mapped out for you — no more feeling your way through life! You're in a vision incubator. Like a baby in a protected area, God will release you for ministry when you are fully developed to handle your calling. Sometimes, we don't realize the fullness of what our lives consist of in our immature state. But if we are in the company of others who are aware of where we are headed, their influence may help to stir us in the right direction. You were made to create something on earth. Whether it be to share peace, encourage others, pastor a church, or originate inventions, you were designed to help someone else. The benefit of your ministry will enable others to move forward in life! So when you can say to yourself: "I'm finally doing what I was created to do" and know it with confidence, you will experience true contentment— one that only comes from God. God wants to share His desire for your life with you. He isn't keeping secrets. He wants you to discover who you are and grow in it. *Do you know what you were called to do* on earth? What gifts and talents do you have that can be used to point people to Jesus?

DISCOVERING MY PURPOSE

Between the ages of eighteen and nineteen, I began singing in the choir, ushering, and leading praise and worship. I absolutely loved singing. I practically sing every day, and I mean **e v e r y d a y**. Music moves you spiritually, emotionally, and physically. It causes you to reflect and change your mindset, as well as things in your life. It's very powerful, just like an elevator ride. It can cause you to go way up or way down. So, we have to choose the right music to listen to.

One day, while in choir rehearsal, I was faithfully learning my part in the Alto section. My cousin, who was also the choir director, approached me and asked me to lead a song entitled "Lift up Your Head." I accepted this opportunity and began to listen to it over and over, in preparation for Sunday's service. I studied the Scripture to understand what the song was saying, according to the Word of God. I asked the Lord to help me push past my shyness, and allow the Holy Spirit to use me to minister to the people in the audience.

Ultimately, I closed my eyes that Sunday morning, and I sang to God as if it was a one-on-one experience. I tuned everyone out so that I could focus on Him. And when I did this, all of the fear, anxiety, nervousness dissipated, as it was just the Lord and me.

"Lift up your heads, you gates; lift them up, you ancient doors, that the King of glory may come in."

— PSALMS 24:19

Soon afterward, I began to pray and seek the Lord regarding what He wanted me to do in the Kingdom. I recognized that I had many gifts, but I wanted to know what my calling was. And one day, in my dad's basement,

I prayed. I prayed until I heard the Lord speak. He told me that I was called to be a preacher and a prophet. And although those two callings were revealed at that moment, little did I know, that there was more to my life than those two titles.

There are many facets to who we are, and we can't be limited by one area of gifting. As the years went by, I began to discover life's journey of finding normal. When I found my way to intimacy with my Father, He opened up my book and revealed my life story, one component at a time. And this is not the end, as there is more to come! There are deeper roots and higher heights that I have yet to obtain, as this will continue throughout my lifetime.

"May be able to comprehend with all saints what is the breadth, and length, and depth, and height..."

— EPHESIANS 3:18

But in that initial moment, I was scared, so I immediately got up from the floor. I was afraid because I was still nervous about being in front of people. As a little girl, I was always shy and bashful. I never felt confident about myself. And I did not want to be seen in front of people. I would often go places with others so that I didn't draw any extra attention to me. However, I didn't know at the time that this was a form of pride.

What is pride? Pride is preferring self-will over God's will. So, being afraid to draw attention to myself, regardless of it being God's will, is a form of pride. It is a selfish way of expressing that because I don't want anyone looking at me, I'm not going to do God's will. So, as a result, I began to pray for God to help me become more comfortable in front of people. I wanted to learn how to be a leader. I had to realize that I wasn't doing the work myself, but that He was doing the work through me as a vessel for His glory. So this required a total self-denial. I had to deny myself gratification from the things that I wanted to do with my life versus His plan for my life— the plan that originated before my inception in my mother's womb.

God has a way of showing you who you are, even when you don't realize it. You may recognize that you're a leader when you wind up being the head of the pack without even trying to lead! You may not be trying to control things, but because God has blessed you with the wisdom and tools lead effectively, it may come naturally to you. So be who God has called you to be. Be bold! Be confident! Never dim your light, and let it shine bright so that others may see! Arise and pursue your purpose!

"Write the vision And make it plain on tablets, that he may run who reads it…"

— HABAKKUK 2:2

LIFE BEFORE CHRIST

When I got saved, I was very excited about my new life. I felt so different and wanted to tell everybody about my new walk with the Lord. I wanted everyone to experience what I experienced. I felt such a deep peace and joy within. This feeling couldn't compare to anything I felt when I was living according to the world's standards before I got saved. Before Christ, I enjoyed partying and drinking, without a care in the world. But when I got saved, there was a difference— a real difference. This relationship with the Lord was the best feeling! It paled in comparison to what I labeled as being fun.

Because I was raised in a Christ-centered home that was built on the foundation of following the Word of God, there were certain things that my parents wouldn't allow us to indulge in. As we grew older, we had a little more liberty, but still realized that there were rules we had to abide by.

Those who knew me as sweet little innocent Crystal didn't know that I had my moments where I didn't do everything right. But as a sinner, this is our nature. At that time, I indulged in a life of sin because I didn't have the Holy Spirit living on the inside to warn me of the traps that the devil set to destroy my life. I had no conviction, and no one to answer to besides my dad. But I knew the Hand of God was on my life, in spite of my actions.

"For I know that good itself does not dwell in me, that is, in my sinful nature. For I have the desire to do what is good, but I cannot carry it out."

— ROMANS 7:18

"Surely I was sinful at birth, sinful from the time my mother conceived me."

— PSALM 51:5

On one particular night, I knew the angels of the Lord were protecting me. It was a weekend night, and my friends and I were on our way to the club. I was drinking in my white Buick that my dad purchased for me, the summer before my senior year in high school. I was so excited about this car, as it was a surprise! And on that one particular night that I drove my new car with my friends, we were blasting the music on the way to the club. I was excited and ready to hang out with my friends, dance, and meet guys— typical actions of teenagers! In North Carolina, the railroad tracks have blinking lights that let you know when a train is coming. But because I'd been drinking, along with the music being loud, I couldn't hear my friends trying to let me know that a train was coming. So as we rolled over the tracks, I happened to look in my rearview mirror and saw that a train was coming. So, I was able to get off the tracks and dodge the oncoming train in time! When I turned down the music, after realizing what had happened, my friends immediately told me that they were trying to warn me about the train all along! And in that short moment, I was grateful, but at the same time, I was still ready to get my party on, not fully realizing that moments ago could have been the end of my life. But looking back on that moment, I am grateful. I knew that the prayers of the righteous covered me. It was not my time to leave. It was nothing but the grace of God that enabled me to be here. There were many occasions when the weapon of premature death sought to consume me, but did not prevail.

"The effectual fervent prayer of a righteous man availeth much."

— JAMES 5:16

ADDICTIONS

What has control over your life? Addiction is a psychological and physical inability to stop consuming a chemical, drug, activity, or substance, even though it causes psychological and physical harm. Merriam-Webster defines addiction as "a compulsive, chronic, physiological or psychological need for a habit-forming substance, behavior, or activity having harmful physical, psychological, or social effects and typically causing well-defined symptoms (such as anxiety, irritability, tremors, or nausea)."

From a Biblical standpoint, addictions refer to you being enslaved by your own self-will. It is our personal responsibility to ensure that we don't open up unhealthy doors that may not be easy to shut. At the time of decision making, you may not be aware that opening a door could form a habit. However, this is why praying is essential. And if you haven't formed that relationship with the Lord in order to receive guidance, let's begin today. Some things we learn by others informing us of the repercussions. Other times, we may witness the harmful effects of a decision that developed into a habit. When such behaviors become second nature, it becomes very hard to break away from its harmful effects. When we indulge in unhealthy behaviors on a consistent basis, it can easily turn into an addiction that was triggered by life's extremities. However, the Bible gives us hope. It informs us that freedom and slavery are a choice that we can make for ourselves.

> "So, since we're out from under the old tyranny, does that mean we can live any old way we want? Since we're free in the freedom of God, can we do anything that comes to mind? Hardly. You know well enough from your own experience that there are some acts of so-called freedom that destroy freedom. Offer yourselves to sin, for instance, and it's your last free act. But offer yourselves to the ways of God, and the freedom never quits. All your lives you've let sin tell you what to do. But thank God you've started listening to a new master, one whose commands set you free to live openly in his freedom!"
>
> — ROMANS 6:15-18

God holds our actions to a high moral standard. However, He knows that we are easily susceptible to enslavement, not realizing it by the courses of action that we take. Furthermore, He knows that we are unable to break free from the tight grip of strongholds on our own.

Alcohol Addiction

In high school, I consumed alcohol for the first time. At the time, I didn't realize that drinking would later become a major stronghold that the devil continuously used to keep me in bondage. My first taste of alcohol was not good at all, but my body's response to it was life-changing, but in a negative way. Drinking allowed me to be the "bold Crystal" that I always wanted to be. The enemy of my soul wanted me to embrace an unhealthy means of achieving a state of boldness. And although its effects were temporary, this method led to a slow demise. But the Holy Spirit stepped in and eradicated this counterfeit method by taking full residence within me. When He entered in, I experienced His boldness through me.

Commercial ads and most movies portray alcohol and drugs as casual things to engage in. It may start off as casual fun, as people refer to it as social drinking. But when it becomes their god and is substituted for the only true and living God, it becomes an idol.

There were many stages of my life where alcohol was my best friend. I woke up drinking and went to bed drinking. I carried it in a juice bottle in my purse to sip on throughout the day, and no one knew. I used it to numb the pain of unresolved issues that were too painful to think about, and too difficult to resolve. So, I thought I needed this substance to numb the pain. Numbness is temporary, and as soon as it wears off, you find that the pre-existing pain is still there. I needed THE ONLY, all-powerful, and loving God to rescue me from self-sabotaging myself. I was killing myself slowly.

Overcoming Addictions

Many of us have addictions— things we do that have power over our actions and behaviors, which can affect our relationships, career, and other critical elements of our lives. Common addictions include: food, drugs, social media, pornography, and sex.

These are real-life issues that real people face every day. And sometimes, it takes someone's story to help us overcome. *How did you make it out of captivity? Are you free?* Anything that we use in place of seeking God will only be a temporary fix that could result in a permanent problem.

Everything requires maintenance. We may wake up one day and say to ourselves, "That's it! This is the last day! No more…!" and be okay for a few days, weeks, months, or even years! But if something happens that takes you by surprise, you may begin to feel overwhelmed. And with anxious thoughts racing through your head, calming down can be challenging. *Do you pray, call someone for help, or go back to the bad addiction that you're comfortable with? Do you have enough faith to know that if we pray that God will rescue us?* God's supernatural rescue overpowers every temporary, natural quick fix.

> "Weeping may remain for a night, but rejoicing comes in the morning."
>
> — PSALM 30:5

Your morning can happen at any time of the day! You may be in your darkest moment, feeling all alone. And even with people around, it feels like you're in a room by yourself. You may feel like no one understands or can feel what you're dealing with. *Don't they see me? Can they identify with my pain? What am I going to do?* Anxiety can come when something happens, and you are unsure of its effects. In such moments, something can trigger your emotion and bring you back to the scenario in your mind of how going back to your addiction can relieve the pressure you're under.

To fuel an addiction, you have to feed it over and over. Once is never enough. God's plan is for us to be made whole, and as long as we stay connected to Him, regardless of what we are dealing with, He will fight our battles. God's resolution does not harm you; it brings life and produces fruit. You will see those benefits in your life, as well as many others.

Triggers can activate suppressed emotions. To understand someone better, consider observing them throughout different seasons of their life. Although this can be helpful, we must be careful to see them with an unbiased view— the way God sees them— because man looks on the outward appearances, but God looks at the heart.

> "The LORD does not look at the things man looks at. Man looks at the outward appearance, but the LORD looks at the heart."
>
> — 1 SAMUEL 16:7

The heart is the depth of our emotions. This is the compartment from which we react and express what's inside of us. We are not a product of how we react in the physical; that's not who we are. It's what's in the heart of man that determines the character. Your reputation is developed by how people see you and view your actions. Your character is built upon the discipline of responding to situations properly so that your actions won't be misinterpreted. People may hold your actions captive and keep you in remembrance of your failures. However, God sees, loves, forgives, and remembers them no more.

> "You will again have compassion on us; you will tread our sins underfoot and hurl all our iniquities into the depths of the sea."
>
> — MICAH 7:19

> "For I will be merciful toward their iniquities, and I will remember their sins no more."
>
> — HEBREWS 8:12

How To Be Free From Addictions:

1. Acknowledge it and confess it. Take ownership of its hold on you.
2. Relinquish your rights over your life.
3. Let God take over the battle and surrender.
4. Ask for help! Go to someone you respect, who also has knowledge of healing and deliverance.
5. Stay accountable to your pastor, leader, mentor, etc.
6. Most importantly, develop a closer relationship with God through prayer and studying the Word of God. And stay close

to others who are living addiction free. Your atmosphere will produce and maintain change.

Prayer To Break Addictions

My Beloved Father, I come to You for help. It is my desire to be free, even when my actions don't dictate this. I give myself to You. I relinquish my rights to control my life from this day forward. I repent for the abuse that I have caused my body up until this point. I ask that You forgive me and bring healing to the areas that have caused me to lean unto my own understanding. I acknowledge that You sent Your son Jesus to sacrifice His life so that I don't have to live in captivity any longer. Today, I choose freedom from this habit. This stronghold has been weakened and will no longer be a weak area for me. Your strength is made perfect in my weakness. You are my strength. You are my peace. You are my strong-tower. You are my defense. And today, is the beginning of my walk of freedom! AMEN!

NEW LIFE WITH CHRIST

At the age of seventeen, I was so grateful that God spared my life. After spending an entire year of partying and hanging out with friends, I realized that this was not the life that I wanted. I saw its effects in a short span of time and did not see it ending well for me, especially at the rate I was going. My life was headed in a downward spiral. But I'm grateful for the safety net of prayer and the promises of God. Soon afterward, I rededicated my life back to Christ.

"For no matter how many promises God has made, they are "Yes" in Christ. And so through him, the "Amen" is spoken by us to the glory of God."

— 2 CORINTHIANS 1:20

"God is not a man, so he does not lie. He is not human, so he does not change his mind. Has he ever spoken and failed to act? Has he ever promised and not carried it through?"

— NUMBERS 23:19

When you live life recklessly, not realizing that at any given moment, your life can be taken from you, you may be blinded to the value of your life. God has blessed us with one opportunity to achieve all that we were sent here to do. If you look at the hours in a day, the days in the week, the weeks in a month, and the months in a year, you can see just how fast time is zooming by. We don't have time to waste. We never have time to waste! *How productive are you with your time?* I made plans with my life, but a lot of those plans fell through because I was not disciplined enough as a young child to complete them. But what I love about God is that when I rededicated my life back to Him and decided to move forward with purpose, things began to progress quickly, as if time was never lost. Things began to move as soon as I finally made my mind up.

FULFILL YOUR PURPOSE

At the age of forty, I am so grateful to be able to write this book and complete some of the things that I never thought I'd be able to do. It is only by the grace of God that He has enabled me to be disciplined in order to accomplish my goals. And although I have many more to accomplish, I am fired up and ready to succeed!

The only thing in life that's stopping us from completing the things that we start is ourselves. We have to eliminate distractions. *What will you allow to stand in the way of completing what God has given you to start?*

You were created to change something! Your life has meaning!

"But you are a chosen people, a royal priesthood, a holy nation, God's special possession, that you may declare the praises of him who called you out of darkness into his wonderful light."

— 1 PETER 2:9

I had to remove all competing forces and realize that it was time for a change. One day, I woke up tired of the same routine and decided to move forward.

At the time, my normal routine as a high school teenager consisted of styling hair after school during the week and on weekends. Styling hair was my source of income. I often used my money to go shopping and to have fun partying on the weekends. Being raised in a Christian home, my dad only allowed me to go out on the weekends if I promised to go to church on Sunday mornings. I enjoyed church as a little girl, but I swayed from it as I got older because my heart was not in it. I loved singing in the choir and listening to music! That's what drew me to church. But I often thought to myself— there has to be more to life than this! The expected normal routine was to graduate from high school, go to college, get a job, get married, have children, and live happily ever after. But I realized that life wasn't that simple; things weren't coming that easy for me.

KNOW WHEN IT'S TIME TO MOVE FORWARD

My five years in the Carolinas had come to an end. My dad decided it was time to move back to Baltimore. His assignment in ministry had been completed, and it was time for him to go. I was so excited because I felt like it would be a fresh start for me back in my hometown, where my friends and family were. But the only thing is, I didn't realize that everything had changed before I left. I had lost contact with most of my friends, and there were so many new faces at my church that I attended. At this point in my life, school was over. I graduated from high school in North Carolina. So, when I moved back to Baltimore, it was time for me to finally do something with my life. Therefore, I decided to attend TESST Technology Institute with one of my cousins.

In college, I majored in office computer applications. The most exciting part about attending college was learning how to type. I thought it was so fascinating to be able to type on the computer and not have to look at the keys. I also learned how to work all of the applications on the computer, such as Microsoft Office, Excel, Access, and PowerPoint. I was able to create spreadsheets, format letters, and was qualified to be an administrative assistant. This was something that I always had an interest in because I liked the idea of going to work and dressing up. I always admired the corporate America atmosphere, so I was thrilled when I received my first real job as a payment processor. Processing payments and doing data entry were easy, but I often got bored because I completed my work so fast. So, most of the time, I had nothing left to do. And for the amount of work I was doing, my paycheck didn't seem worth it. So, I finally decided to go to school for hair in order to pursue my career as a cosmetologist.

My new normal consisted of working during the day and attending school in the evenings and on the weekends. This was a very difficult schedule for me to maintain, so I decided to finish my apprenticeship under my aunt in her salon. And after taking the test numerous times, I passed it and received my license in cosmetology. Things were going well, as I began to accomplish things both in the natural and in the spiritual.

MY SPIRITUAL DEVELOPMENT

At the age of twenty-one, I preached my first sermon. My sermon was titled "Too Much is at Stake." I preached from Matthew 13:1-23. Preaching was an act of faith because I was so terrified to preach in front of so many people, especially for the first time. I was so nervous; I couldn't eat or sleep. I simply wanted God to take over. And just before I preached, I sat on the pulpit and prayed, asking the Lord to completely take over. And that's exactly what He did. It felt so natural once I opened up my mouth. I allowed the Lord to take over and speak through me. I will never forget the moment when it felt like fire was on top of my head, and I recognized that I was not in control. And that's exactly how God wants us to be. He wants us to be in a place where we submit to His will and get ourselves out of the way so that He can take over and change lives. People need to hear the Good News in the midst of a world full of chaos and evil. Someone needs to open their mouth and spread the gospel of Jesus Christ, proclaiming it everywhere they go, so that others can see that there is hope in Christ.

After preaching my first sermon, I was excited, yet overwhelmed. I didn't know that so much would transpire after accepting the call to preach. *Does accepting this call exempt me from disappointments in my life? Was my life limited to just preaching behind a pulpit? Would my life be perfect now? Would I make any mistakes?* I quickly received the answers to these questions. No, life would not be free of disappointments! No, I would not be perfect! And yes, I will still make mistakes. At the time, I didn't realize that after receiving salvation, there's still a process for dealing with internal issues from your past. Generational challenges, as well as current issues, would still need to be properly addressed. Salvation doesn't void you of the need to address any presenting challenges. The most difficult stage of my walk with God was dealing with the recovery process after sin. I was my worst enemy when it came to this. I made mistakes based upon unresolved issues from my past. I didn't realize that I was still deeply affected by certain things in my past. I was not at a place where I was fully confident in who God created me to be. In addition, my self-esteem was poor; I didn't truly love myself. I did not know my worth, and because of this, I settled in many different ways, especially in my relationships. My relationships were my greatest downfall.

Seven years after I answered the call of God to preach and be a disciple, I got pregnant out of wedlock. I was in love, or so I thought. My dad always told me that I wore my heart on my sleeve, so I guess that's why it was so easy for me to open up my heart. *But was it love or the idea of love?* Three years after my divorce, I entered into another relationship, after overcoming one of the most difficult seasons I ever had to face. I was married and divorced within two years, and experienced a miscarriage within the confines of that marriage. That was the hardest season of my life, or so I thought. As I kept living, I realized that I had to break that unhealthy vicious cycle of coming into covenant with people who weren't connected to my destiny.

MY SPIRITUAL BLESSINGS

At that time, my goddaughter, Khadijah, moved in with me. She called me "Ma" back then, and to this day, I still say, "My daughter." At the age of 25, I developed a relationship with a beautiful soul— inside and out. Though faced with many challenges in her life, most of which she had no control over, her story inspired me to keep moving. When we first met, I mentored her on the weekends. But over time, we grew close, and God told me to adopt her. It was such a joyous time, as we had so much fun together!

On Mondays, we watched movies and ate popcorn together. During the week, she assisted me at the salon as my shampoo assistant; she was very skilled, and my clients loved her vibrant personality. After working all week, our highlight was going to the mall to shop! It was such an exciting period of time for me, as I had something to look forward to with her. She gave me a reason to push past the things I was going through. She viewed me as an example, and I didn't want to let her down. As she looked up to me, I looked up to God. I pulled on Him for my goddaughter's sake, not realizing that I would receive the very thing that I needed. God gave me the wisdom I needed to help impart to her what was needed at that time in her life. God gave me someone to be accountable to and responsible for. While I poured into her, God poured into me. It was like a pitcher of water that flowed from God to me, and through me to my goddaughter. It was a beautiful flow that blessed us both. We were what each other needed during this challenging period in both of our lives. The interesting thing was that I was not fully aware of all that I had to offer, but I poured into her everything that I had within me. With the strength and wisdom that God gave me, I was so privileged to play a key role in her life.

From this experience, I learned that I had much more potential than I thought. It's important for us to understand that we have the potential to be a leader and an effective influencer. God has somebody who can benefit from what we have on the inside, regardless of what phase of our lives we're in. We don't have to wait. We can release as we grow, as God gives us more to give.

"He cuts off every branch in me that bears no fruit, while every branch that does bear fruit he prunes so that it will be even more fruitful."

— JOHN 15:2

Needless to say, this was a very pivotal point in her life, as well as in mine. I needed her just as much as she needed me. God used her as a means to help me push past the pain of my past. And while that was not my present focus, I was able to receive healing at the same time. Our connection helped us both to heal. Prior to our meeting, she attained a wonderful achievement of becoming a teenage author, whose story was published in the book "Teenage Blues." I was so astonished by her writing piece that I could hardly put it down. She is also a homeowner, singer, songwriter, and celebrity hairstylist. I celebrate her success and continue to pray that she fulfills every vision that God has created her to achieve.

My son, who is eleven years old, has been my inspiration to move forward and pursue my dreams. What I viewed as the most shameful and depressing time in my life, produced a wonderful blessing— my son,

Joshua. "They that sow in tears shall reap in joy" is of one of my favorite scriptures. I cried almost every day because of my guilt and state of mind. I wanted to have a child, but not under those circumstances. And although I was twenty-eight, I didn't feel that I was prepared because my pregnancy wasn't planned. Though it caught me by surprise, I was still excited at the same time. The most exciting part was going to the doctor and watching my son grow over several months. I experienced a scare at five and a half months when I went into labor, but the grace of God allowed the doctor the ability to stop my contractions. And although I was on bed rest for three and a half months, it was totally worth it for the bundle of joy I received. Joshua is a lively, creative, smart, and inquisitive young man who loves to write, play the piano, pray, read, and of course— play video games! And I wouldn't trade him for anything in the world!

REFLECT/ JOURNAL

RESOURCES FOR CHAPTER TEN

Refer to the Strategies of Finding Normal
Section: "Overcome Offense"

Refer to the 30 Day Devotional
Day 16: "No Longer Hidden"
(*Available November 2021*)

10

KEEP MOVING

*A*s Believers, we have the Spirit of God on the inside, and there is no failure in Him. What man views as flawed, God sees as an opportunity for Him to be glorified in our lives. It's a win-win situation because our Father already planned it out!

Sometimes in life, things just won't run smoothly. We have to acknowledge that and be okay with it. Most of us just want to wake up every day, go out to handle all of our daily activities, come home, relax, and then go to bed. Well, some of our days don't particularly go that way, so we have to know that despite the obstacles we face, whether good or bad, things will be okay. *Do we stop making forward progression because a day came and went? Was it so disappointing that you felt like it was the end of the world?* Celebrate during the good days, but learn and grow from the bad. But no matter what— keep moving!

ADDRESS THE ROOT

I remember countless times when as soon as something negative came across my doorstep, I would retreat and shut everyone out. For many years, I didn't understand what those actions were, but I knew how I felt. Those were the times when I couldn't get out of the bed, and I didn't want to live. And whenever someone left my life or if things didn't go as I expected, it would trigger those actions. This depression was like a sitting duck, waiting for something to push its button. It was a trap. And it seemed like no matter what was going on in my life, I kept falling for it. I didn't know how to break free of it, but I so deeply wanted to.

All of my relationships throughout the years have suffered from it or ended because of my actions. These actions were not done intentionally to cause any harm, but I simply couldn't fight the pain I felt inside. One day, it was recommended that I go to see a therapist to learn why I was so mentally challenged at this point in my life. I was diagnosed with severe depression, and even though I found out the cause of those feelings, having that knowledge didn't make those feelings go away.

Because I am a born-again Believer, I thought that I was doing something wrong. I felt bad for feeling this way because I thought that everything would eventually be okay after getting saved and starting a ministry. I fell into the pattern of getting overly involved in ministry and extracurricular activities— anything to stay busy and keep my mind off of what had me depressed! Oftentimes, the busyness would occur after I spent days in bed with the lights out— crying and not eating! This was what I called therapy, and I thought I felt better. But while taking what I thought was a proactive step, I was really damaging myself. And I didn't learn of its effects until several years down the road. Ignoring the issue doesn't solve the problem; it makes matters worse. This was a stronghold that had a grip on me, and I didn't know how to deal with it. I didn't realize the severity of the matter, and that's why I wasn't aware of the steps to take to be free.

> "For the weapons of our warfare are not carnal, but mighty through God to the pulling down of strongholds; casting down imaginations, and every high thing that exalts itself against the knowledge of God and bringing into captivity every thought to the obedience to Messiah."
>
> — 2 CORINTHIANS 10:4-5

The fight was in my mind. And a result of recognizing that, I wanted to admit myself in a hospital to be medicated so that I wouldn't have to deal with my pain. Pain comes and goes, but I was managing the pain, not healing what was causing the pain.

I wanted to be free, but did not surrender every area to God. But the truth is, I wasn't aware that I hadn't fully surrendered yet. But I quickly learned that deliverance sometimes takes time. All things aren't addressed at once. Attachments that were formed throughout life can still linger, even though you may be physically out of the situation. Your thoughts and those deep emotional wounds in your soul may have formed the core of who you are. But no matter what took place, you can still be free.

"Therefore if the Son makes you free, you shall be free indeed."

— JOHN 8:36

KEEP GROWING

It would be easy for a teacher to give you a test, and then provide you with the correct answers for the ones that weren't answered incorrectly. A good teacher wants to walk you through the answer to tell you where you may have made a mistake, while showing you the necessary steps to arrive at your answer. And despite the way the question was presented, you can use some of the principles you learned from the previous answer to help you find a solution to other problems. God wants the same thing for us. He wants us to learn and grow, so we can teach others how to navigate through life's situations.

The shortest route is not always the best route. Sometimes it takes time to address everything that's going on. *But what if you thought you surrendered your all?* I was so discouraged when I realized that I still had unresolved issues. It was self-righteous of me to believe that I had it all together, even though I thought I was okay. I thought to myself, "Well, I've been through some things, I made it out, and now I'm living my life." The phrase "I'm good" is something I would often say, even though I didn't always mean it. But when you are accustomed to religious environments where not being truthful about how you feel is the norm, it then becomes your norm. Therefore, it was difficult for me to admit when something was going on. I felt like doing everything right would get me closer to God and that it would help me appear as if I had it all together, especially in front of those I looked up to.

> "For by grace, you have been saved through faith, and that not of yourselves; it is the gift of God, not of works, lest anyone should boast."
>
> — EPHESIANS 2:8-9

At that time, there were people God sent in my life who I looked up to for support. They were my safe haven! God sent people who would listen, give wise counsel when needed, and pray. While living in a world where you can't always let your guard down, it was a blessing to have people in my corner who I could be transparent with. Your transparency isn't safe everywhere, and no one can take the best care for your heart like God. So, when He sends someone on His behalf to care for your heart, it's truly a blessing. And as the Scripture says, we must be careful to guard our hearts.

> "Above all else, guard your heart, for everything you do flows from it."
>
> — PROVERBS 4:23

REFLECT/ JOURNAL

RESOURCES FOR CHAPTER ELEVEN

Refer to the Strategies of Finding Normal
Section: "Plan Your Life"

Refer to the 30 Day Devotional
Day 26: "Don't Second Guess Yourself/
Doubt Has To Go"
(*Available November 2021*)

When you're not focused on the prize, you may become distracted by things that happen around you. You may second guess the truth because it doesn't appear to be what you've envisioned.

Let's practice reacting to the following list of words below. After prayer, what is the first thought that comes to mind after you read each of these words? How can you apply them to your life?

Mountain
Rainbow
Desert
Storm
Valley

11

BE CONFIDENT ABOUT YOUR VISION

*D*o you have a vision for your life? If the answer is yes, then this is good! Write out the vision for your life in a few sentences. But before you do, utilize these questions to help you!

- What do you see yourself doing in the next couple of years? Is this something that you could wake up every day and be joyful about doing?

- Have you prayed about the direction your life should take? And what did you sense God telling you? What evidence did He reveal to confirm what you sensed?

- Will your vision solve a problem in the world? How will it have an impact on society?

Once you're finished answering these questions, consider combining them to form a vision statement for your life. Sometimes, when looking for direction, you have to start somewhere. And you may have heard this before, but the answer lies within.

DISCOVER VISION EARLY

As you begin to talk, pray, and meditate, you will begin to understand that everything you are supposed to do on earth is already inside you. God put it in you before you were born so that no one can take the credit for forming you into what they want you to be. Even though we have parents, mentors, and teachers, as well as those who mean well, it's important that they pray and ask God for direction when advising others about the direction they should take.

It is very important for parents to start observing what's inside of their children. They may not specifically know their child's purpose, but they can start by paying attention to the things that their child loves to do.

Gifts and talents come from God. Some things come through the DNA in our bloodline. Some traits may be good, whereas others may be bad. But when you have a gift from God, we must be careful to use it to glorify Him. If not, it can potentially bring damage to the world and those around us.

Consider the gift of music. Someone that is gifted to sing and play instruments could send a mixed message and steer someone in the wrong direction. Instead, that gift should be used to point others to Jesus and not away from Him! Music has significant influence, as words are spoken into the atmosphere through a melody and rhythm that is pleasing to the ears. But regardless of its sound or delivery, words bring life. The Bible declares that life and death are in your tongue, so if things are being sung or spoken, it will eventually bring forth life or death.

SPEAK LIFE

It's important to make sure that we regularly speak life over our future. Even if what you see in your present doesn't look like what you desire in your future, you speak positively about it. Daily motivations and affirmations can be used for self-motivation. Reading the Word of God should always be a priority so that you will know what God declares about your future. Inspirational books can help edify you and keep your mind focused on positive movements and productivity. Also, attending workshops and seminars can teach you about forward progression— spiritually, naturally, and professionally. There are so many resources that can help you move in a positive direction versus a direction that God did not intend. It's our responsibility to ensure that we've exhausted all possibilities when it comes to the health of lives. You may be discouraged today, but do not allow discouragement and discontentment to stop you from making plans.

MAKE YOUR PLAN

Plans help you see your life from a different perspective; you will be able to see your future before it gets here. And this is what we call faith! The Bible says that faith is the substance of things hoped for and the evidence of things not seen. In other words, when you believe in something so strongly before it happens, you are able to take the necessary steps, as if it has already happened. This is so vitally important for progress in your life. God fashioned and designed us with a measure of faith. All of us have faith. And even though some people have higher faith levels, your faith can grow based on what you're feeding yourself.

"You are what you eat" is a popular phrase that's used. Whatever you feed yourself is what will lead you throughout your life. So, if you constantly stay around negative people that are stuck in the place that they're in, then this pattern of negative speaking may affect you, as well! Hoping and wishing is not enough. Eventually, you have to put on your skates if you want to skate.

Remember, progress takes time. Crawl before you walk. Walk before you run. And at some point throughout the journey, you may need to add extra support. So, get a motor on your seat. Put your skates on. Get a skateboard. Get a bike. Get on a treadmill, or do whatever you have to do to make progress at a steady pace! Some things may need to be fast-tracked. And what I love about God is that He shows us in the Bible that He is a God who can restore the years that were taken from us. God may choose to do this as a bonus, to move you ahead and make up for time wasted. As teenagers, young adults, or even older adults, we may have wasted time at some point in our lives. And sometimes, it's good to acknowledge the past mistakes, but we must learn to move forward, starting with today.

MOVE FORWARD

Today, you must make a conscious effort to move forward from a place of despondency. *Are you ready for a change?* Create a change! Make the change that you want to see. Don't depend on anybody else to do it for you. God has given you the power to create the life that He planned for you to have. There's no need to be sad and depressed about what has been. Use what you have to get what belongs to you.

You deserve the best. God created you in His likeness and His image. So, everything about you is good. I know you may think to yourself, "But I'm flawed, and I have all of these issues that I can't break! I have hurt others and even myself. So, how am I good?" But God is not flawed. And our flaws open the opportunity for Him to be glorified. He can turn a negative situation around to work out in your favor.

APPRECIATE YOU

As a child, I thought of my lips as a flaw. That was one thing that I didn't like about myself. I got picked on in middle school about how large my lips were. But now, society has changed so much! People get lip injections to make their lips bigger. This demonstrates how what we may see as a flaw may be desired in another's eyes. We may think something is bad, but others may wish they had what we don't appreciate. Therefore, it's important to be grateful and appreciate who we are and how we're made.

Embrace who you are— inside and out! And if there are things that need to be changed, work on them daily, with the help of the Lord. Consult the Word of God and other positive influences in order to develop in a positive manner.

BE BOLD & BELIEVE

Timing is everything. There have been many times in my life where I started projects and did not finish them. Loss of motivation, failure, discouragement from others, and lack of support, are some of the painful feelings I've experienced. But in the last seven to eight years of my life, I stepped out on faith to accomplish things that I would not have been bold enough to do in the past. I didn't know if they would work. I didn't even know if I could accomplish it, but I did it anyway. I was bold because I was secure in who I was. And that security gave me the confidence I needed to take action. And over time, I continued to build my faith. I built my faith to the point where I felt like I could accomplish anything!

Throughout my life, I've been the one who helped others plan and organize their events behind the scenes. But in 2017, I did something different. I stepped out on faith and planned my first hair and fashion show. I hired a fashion show coordinator, pulled together a team, and planned my first show! And on the day of the show, I was so shocked! There was a room full of people in the audience! To this day, it still brings tears to my eyes when I think about it, as I never would've thought that my event would be that successful. That was truly an example of me putting my faith to the test. I was super excited, and I thought to myself, "If I can do this, I can do anything!" And even though things were a little challenging behind the scenes, we pulled through it. But best of all, no one in the audience could tell! It all came together in the end, and that's all that matters. So I said to myself, "Now that I can do this, I can plan any event that I want, and I know it will be a success!" Sometimes we don't begin because we don't believe in what God has invested in us. Anything that we focus on long enough to plan, strategize, and put together, has the potential to be successful. Oftentimes, it's just a matter of us believing that it can be done! We must be bold enough to believe that our visions can be fulfilled with God's help!

HAVE VISION

When we dig deeper, we can see what the Bible says about having a vision.

> "Where there is no vision, the people perish: but he that keepeth the law, happy is he."
>
> — PROVERBS 29:18

This verse provides so much clarity regarding the way we should handle moving forward in our lives. Without the Word of God, a dream, a vision, or a prophetic word, people will live life recklessly. So, there has to be restraint and careful attention given to making decisions that pertain to our future.

Many can say that they've wasted time giving their attention to things that produced nothing. Unfortunately, the choice that was made didn't manifest the fruit that may have been expected. Imagine if you worked a job for a full year without saving any money. You may have paid bills, but didn't put money on the side to go towards the ultimate plan for your life that you're working on. And based on the state of the current economy, most people live from paycheck to paycheck, trying to make ends meet. *But how do we break this vicious cycle?*

EXAMPLES OF VISIONARIES

In the Bible, we see that Jesus is the perfect example of someone who was raised from birth with a purpose. His purpose can be summarized in John 3:16-17:

> "For God so loved the world that He gave His only begotten Son, that whoever believes in Him shall not perish, but have eternal life. For

FINDING NORMAL

God did not send the Son into the world to judge the world, but that the world might be saved through Him."

— JOHN 3:16-17

Jesus was sent into this world with specific instructions. And there was no room for error because there is no failure in God.

Samson is an example of someone who was born with a purpose, failed, got back up, and kept going until his purpose was fulfilled.

"Again the children of Israel did evil in the sight of the Lord, and the Lord delivered them into the hand of the Philistines for forty years. Now there was a certain man from Zorah, of the family of the Danites, whose name was Manoah; and his wife was barren and had no children. And the Angel of the Lord appeared to the woman and said to her, "Indeed now, you are barren and have borne no children, but you shall conceive and bear a son. Now, therefore, please be careful not to drink wine or similar drink, and not to eat anything unclean. For behold, you shall conceive and bear a son. And no razor shall come upon his head, for the child shall be a Nazirite to God from the womb; and he shall begin to deliver Israel out of the hand of the Philistines."

— JUDGES 13:1-5

Oprah Winfrey is a prime example of a person that wasn't born with a silver spoon in her mouth. She was able to defy all odds and is worth an estimated $3.1 billion. She was born to a teenage single mother and lived in a home that didn't always have running water and electricity.

Ralph Lauren is another example of a cycle-breaker. As a kid, he wore his brother's hand-me-downs, but most likely said to himself, "One day, I want to have my own clothes, so I can make my own statement."

LAUNCH YOUR VISION

One thing I know to be true is that you won't start seeing change until you desire to see it. To see things manifest on the outside, we must allow God to work on us from the inside. This is not always an easy task, as we may think we are okay in some areas that God desires to work on. But when we surrender ourselves to the Lord, who is the Creator of everything, we will see the areas that we need to work on. And this will allow us to be a better person, not just for ourselves, but for others.

Being here on earth is all about building relationships. If you aren't able to build healthy relationships with others, your life cannot progress. We need each other to move forward.

Imagine if you launched the greatest invention of all time, but no one benefited from it because no one purchased your invention. And because there was no use, there was no benefit! So, this is why we know that we need each other. You may have gifts that benefit my life, as I may have gifts that may benefit yours! We all can benefit from being connected to the right people at the right time.

One Body But Many Parts

There is one body, but it has many parts. But all its many parts make up one body. It is the same with Christ. We were all baptized by one Holy Spirit. And so we are formed into one body. It didn't matter whether we were Jews or Gentiles, slaves, or free people. We were all given the same Spirit to drink. So the body is not made up of just one part. It has many parts.

Suppose the foot says, "I am not a hand. So, I don't belong to the body." By saying this, it cannot stop being part of the body. And suppose the ear says, "I am not an eye. So, I don't belong to the body." By saying this, it cannot stop being part of the body. If the whole body were an eye, how could it hear? If the whole body were an ear, how could it smell? God has placed each part in the body just as he wanted it to be. If all the parts were the same, how could there be a body? As it is, there are many parts. But there is only one body.

> The eye can't say to the hand, "I don't need you!" The head can't say to the feet, "I don't need you!" It is just the opposite. The parts of the body that seem to be weaker are the ones we can't do without. The parts that we think are less important we treat with special honor. The private parts aren't shown. But they are treated with special care. The parts that can be shown don't need special care. But God has put together all the parts of the body. And he has given more honor to the parts that didn't have any. In that way, the parts of the body will not take sides. All of them will take care of one another. If one part suffers, every part suffers with it. If one part is honored, every part shares in its joy.
>
> You are the Body of Christ. Each one of you is a part of it.
>
> — 1 CORINTHIANS 12:12-27

As individuals, we are composed of many gifts and talents that have been given to us by God. Each of our gifts helps us, as a whole, to accomplish God's true mission as believers. It's essential that we establish unity and get the work done together, while developing long-lasting, healthy relationships.

REFLECT/ JOURNAL

_____
_____
_____
_____
_____
_____
_____
_____
_____
_____
_____
_____
_____
_____
_____
_____
_____
_____
_____

RESOURCES FOR CHAPTER TWELVE

Refer to the Strategies of Finding Normal
Section: "Forgiveness"

Refer to the 30 Day Devotional
Day 17: "A New Day is Dawning"
(*Available November 2021*)

12

PASS THE BATON

Out of pain, greatness is produced. The more pressure we receive, the more determined we should be to push forward— by any means necessary!

In life, we have to be determined to push past challenging circumstances; we cannot allow them to stop us. Painful circumstances may force you to deal with matters that have nothing to do with your present circumstance. When you're in extreme physical pain, your natural response may be to focus on something else, not the pain at hand. This could help momentarily, but it is not a long-term solution to the pain, as you don't want it to affect the other parts of your body. When we allow one area to take control, it can negatively affect the rest of our bodies and slow down forward movement. Therefore, we should ensure that we have a healthy mindset regarding our response to such situations. It's important for us to understand that pain in one area should never stop us from accomplishing our goals. And although this may require much discipline and restraint to ensure that we don't become stagnant, having that firm mindset is needed. While you're experiencing this, it's perfectly okay to have feelings. Feelings are simply indicators that we're human and that something bothered us, but it's *how* we react to it that makes all the difference.

When the Israelites were in slavery, they experienced intense agony. But as the pressure upon them intensified, the greater they expanded. From this passage, it's essential that we learn to allow our pressure to push us into greater expansion:

"And the children of Israel were fruitful, and increased abundantly, and multiplied, and waxed exceeding mighty, and the land was filled with them.

Now there arose up a new king over Egypt, which knew not Joseph.

And he said unto his people, Behold, the people of the children of Israel are more and mightier than we:

Come on, let us deal wisely with them; lest they multiply, and it come to pass, that, when there falleth out any war, they join also unto our enemies and fight against us, and so get them up out of the land.

Therefore they did set over them taskmasters to afflict them with their burdens. And they built for Pharaoh treasure cities, Pithom and Raamses.

But the more they afflicted them, the more they multiplied and grew. And they were grieved because of the children of Israel."

— EXODUS 1:7-15

A TESTIMONY OF GRACE

As a daughter of the King, my Heavenly Father has given me the attributes and abilities to fulfill my purpose on earth. Everything that He desires for me to be has already been imparted within me since birth. I thank the Lord for blessing me with two wonderful people that He trusted to birth me into this world— Jacob & Exemea Schroeder.

Two Loving Hearts

When I look at the character attributes of my mom and dad, I can see why God chose them as my parents. Both in the natural and in the spirit, they carry attributes that I currently see in myself today. I am thankful for every attribute that was released into me from our Heavenly Father above. My mom's life displayed a beautiful picture of redemption and restoration. I observed her traveling along a journey in search of her true identity, despite losing many things in the natural. But towards the end of her life, she came into the realization of who God created her to be! And although my mother had a very humble and passive personality, she was as bold as a lion whenever the Holy Spirit flowed through her. Both of my parents walked in this grace. My dad had a more outgoing personality, as far as how he interacted with people. He was able to go places and make friends with anyone. He could hold a conversation with any type of person, regardless of cultural differences. He loved everyone the same. My mom was a nurturer; she loved children, and they loved her, too! It made perfect sense that God joined two loving hearts together in marriage, despite their natural separation on earth.

United As One

A month before my mom transitioned, she experienced a powerful dream. This dream took place three years after my dad transitioned. Within the dream, my mom and dad were in a white room ministering together. And based on her description, I believe that it was God's plan for my parents to minister together on earth. But due to unforeseen choices and trials, they were unable to do ministry together, as God desired. And although I never explained my thoughts about this dream to my mom, I believe that God allowed her to experience this for a reason. I truly believe that although my parents were unable to minister together on earth, they will be reconnected together in heaven.

After my parents divorced, they were still friends. Their connection never ended, as I believe they still loved each other deeply. It was as if a piece of my mom left when my dad transitioned. This is how I knew that their two souls were united as one. So, despite their divorce in the natural realm, I sincerely believe they never separated in the spirit. There are many stories where people who've been married for long periods of time transition shortly after the other. And when this happens, it truly shows the depth of their connection.

God's Vision

Both of my parents had a vision from God. They knew exactly what they were designed to do. God gave my dad the vision to start his church Temple of Faith. My mom was given the vision to start her own catering business. My dad was gifted to write poetry, and my mom loved to draw. What a beautiful love story—two creative hearts intertwined! My dad gave his total life for ministry and went to drastic lengths to demonstrate his obedience to His Father in Heaven. He changed many lives through the power of God. My mom— a gentle, delicate soul— had the unique ability to minister to others in a kindhearted way. And whenever my parents were wronged, they didn't retaliate in a harsh matter. They were kind and loving people who were careful not to bring detriment to anyone else's life.

A Testimony of Love

From July 2006 to November 2008, my mom wrote out thirty-three sermon titles and their corresponding Scripture references. But in 2011, my mom became sick with a kidney disease, which led to a downward spiral of many health challenges. Months before she transitioned, she went through a major surgery where she received a heart defibrillator. And while in surgery, her heart stopped several times— but God restored her life! After her recovery, my mom told this testimony several times. And because of this, she vowed to say *yes* to God's call on her life to preach the Gospel of Jesus Christ.

In October of 2013, my mom preached her first sermon. But a few weeks afterward, her health began to fail again. And five months later, she transitioned to be with God. Despite what happened, God graced her to fulfill one aspect of her purpose that she initially ran from due to her fear of man. She didn't believe that she could articulate her words as effectively as others, and was discouraged after being labeled for her challenge with mental instabilities. But despite her despondency, God knew all of her struggles, and His strength was made perfect in her weakness.

"But he said to me, 'My grace is sufficient for you, for my power is made perfect in weakness.' Therefore I will boast all the more gladly about my weaknesses, so that Christ's power may rest on me."

— 2 CORINTHIANS 12:9

She was able to reach beyond the voices that traumatized her from childhood through adulthood and heard her Father's voice from Heaven. His voice began to ring louder and louder, filtering out the voices of fear and defeat. And when she heard His voice in her heart— loud and clear— she accepted His will for her life and responded to the call. It was a call to *obedience*— a call to *purpose*— a call to *freedom*! She truly loved God and rested in the freedom of His Word. And whom the Son sets free, is free indeed— not to be entangled again with the yoke of bondage!

"If the Son, therefore, shall make you free, ye shall be free indeed."

— JOHN 8:36-37

A Testimony of Faith

My dad operated in ministry as a prophet and an apostle. This was not an easy task, as he carried a heavy mantle from the Lord. But despite the many tests, he said *yes*! He was bold and courageous. And regardless of what he faced in life, he kept pushing because he stood for the Word of God. He knew when God spoke, and he never wanted to deviate from that, no matter how much backlash it brought him!

He sacrificed it all— his entire life to the call of God. I saw him heal the sick and raise the dead. He preached and prophesied in dead places. And sometimes, he even received harsh criticism because of it. But no matter what, he stood. He loved serving God. And I am so blessed to have witnessed the highs and lows of it all. It was all beautiful to me. My dad's life of bravery and commitment has always captivated my heart.

My Dad's Transition

Years later, my dad was diagnosed with stage four cancer of the liver. When I heard this news, I was devastated. Accepting that my dad — *my superhero*— had a terminal illness was unbearable, and I couldn't stand to see his health decline.

I'll never forget the day that I went to church and asked God to heal my dad. I prayed so hard on the altar for my dad's healing. And when I finished, the Lord told me that he would not die of this disease. As relieved as I was, I didn't immediately share this information with my dad. I held it in my heart, choosing to trust God's Word over the matter. In the meantime, he went to seek out treatment, but doctors said that there was nothing they could do. He began to change his diet and remained faithful. He never once complained. One day, he came to me and told me about his visit to the hospital. When he got checked out, they told him that his cancer was gone! He told me that the doctors were shaking their heads and knew that it was a miracle! Years later, I finally shared what God told me on the altar. I told my dad that God said he would not die of cancer. My dad was so amazed and grateful to hear this report! But to our surprise, he transitioned three days later, after experiencing a heart attack. And despite the pain of his transition, I celebrated the fact that God remained true to His Word.

The time leading up to my dad's transition was so memorable. I'm grateful that God set the stage and allowed us to share a special time together before his transition. My dad and I saw each other weekly. And because he lived within minutes of my home, I saw him often. One evening, he asked me if he could use my truck to go bowling. Bowling was something he loved to do. He was a part of a bowling league that traveled and played in several competitions. Bowling, along with playing pool with his brothers once a week, was the highlight of my dad's life— they had a tight bond that couldn't be broken! But on that particular evening, I was planning to attend a gospel concert. However, I decided to join my dad and go bowling. And I'm grateful that I did! On several occasions, my dad asked me to go bowling with him; he wanted to introduce me to his bowling buddies. It was a touching moment to hear others say they felt like they already knew me, based on how much my dad talked about me! I remember the conversation we had when he wanted something to eat. He ordered french fries and a soda! I told him I was watching my weight and was not going to eat any french fries. He said, "Oh Crys, you're going to be okay. It's not gonna hurt you!" So, I gave in. I ate the fries. But little did I know, that would be our last meal together. Surprisingly, we didn't even bowl a game that night. It was so touching that we were able to spend that quality time together. The next day, he called me, wanting to talk about the merging of two phone companies. However, I was so focused on doing my schoolwork that I asked him if I could call him back when I finished. He responded, "Sure, no problem. Call me back." And that was the last conversation we had.

To this day, I am truly thankful to have such vivid memories of my dad. I will cherish these wonderful memories forever.

My Mom's Transition

My mom and I lived in the same apartment building for an entire year before she transitioned. This was truly God's doing, as it gave us the opportunity to have a closer bond— closer than we've ever had as mother and daughter. And before she transitioned, we shared so many great memories together!

I remember the last Christmas we spent together. My mom and I cooked, and it was so nice to share that quality time together. My mom was a phenomenal cook. We had a nice spread laid out: turkey, stuffing, yams, collard greens, rolls, potato salad, cabbage, sweet potato pies, cake, and macaroni and cheese. *Oh man, thinking back to this menu makes my mouth water!* My mother was an old school cook— she didn't measure anything! She just simply added additional ingredients, as needed. It was such an honor to cook with her and to spend time with my family, not knowing that two months later, she would transition.

The day of my mom's transition was strange, as I knew there was something wrong. Almost every morning, she called me to say "Good morning" before I left for work. Sometimes, she would even request that I bring her something to eat after I got off. But one particular morning, she didn't call me, which I thought was so strange. So, I called her several times to check on her, but to no avail! I was unable to reach her. Later, I found out that she had transitioned in her sleep. This was a few days before Valentine's Day. The week prior, I bought her an early Valentine's Day gift, not knowing that we wouldn't have time to share that day together. However, God saw fit to ensure that we were able to share precious moments together before her transition.

God is love, and He pays great attention to the details of our lives. Nothing occurs by happenstance. He loves us and knows just how much we can bear. And in those times when we think life is unbearable, we can truly see that His strength is made perfect in our weakness.

Life is short, so try to make the most of it. Gather as many memories as you can! So, I admonish you to forgive and make amends with those that you love. And for those that are difficult to love, pray that God's love will heal your heart and flow through you. Love while you can, and express kindness while you have the opportunity to do so here on earth. Our time here is temporary, but our time with the Lord is eternal! Moments are precious, and will one day become memories in our hearts to share with others.

A Great Celebration

My parents' homegoing services were great celebrations. Even in mourning, I was able to rejoice and experience the joy of the Lord.

Everyone that knows me knows that I love to praise the Lord! And I will never be ashamed of my relationship with my Father.

At my dad's homegoing service, I was determined to praise the Lord, in spite of my emotions or the expectations of others who desired a certain reaction from me. Regardless of their expectations, I continued to praise God! I danced, jumped, and leaped in celebration of a life well-lived — an imprint that was made on this earth, that people are still talking about today!

At my mom's homegoing service, there was a great celebration of worship, as well. The choir sang all of her favorite songs, as we experienced the joy of the Lord. At her service, I was able to share the pulpit with my brother, Tony. We both decided to preach our mother's eulogy, which was a beautiful experience. At first, I was nervous and did not know what to expect or how to react. But as my brother and I walked over to our mother's casket to give her one final look, we said our goodbyes, and then entered the pulpit together to preach. We walked up to the pulpit, ready to preach the sermons our mother didn't have an opportunity to preach. We experienced such peace, knowing that we were able to fulfill a task that she desired to complete one day.

After experiencing both homegoing services, I knew that my parents were finally at peace and had entered into eternal rest. And having that comfort surpassed every stream of emotion that flowed during that time — even to this day! May the legacy of Jacob and Exemea Schroeder continue to live on.

My parents' lives will always be my testimony of love and faith in God. They were blessed with vision and creativity. And although they didn't have the opportunity to venture into all of the plans that were on their hearts to do, their legacies shall live on. I will carry the torch of their legacies and follow the path that God has laid before me. I have my own journey to walk, and I will continue this path with my Father, as I finish my assignment here on earth.

AFTER YOU'VE CRIED A RIVER

After my mother's homegoing service, I continued to move forward with my son Joshua's birthday party the next day. He was turning four years old! His actual birthday was on the day of her service, but I decided to have his party on the following day.

Due to the magnitude of it all, my dear friends paid for me to stay in a hotel because they simply wanted me to rest. I pulled up to the hotel room alone, went up the elevator, and put the key into the door. After taking two or three steps, I fell on the floor and began to weep. It was at this moment that I said to myself, "I would've never thought I would live to see the day when both of my parents were gone!" I didn't feel like I had the opportunity to truly mourn my father's transition, so at that moment in the hotel, I mourned both of my parents. One of the songs that helped me get through that weekend was the song "Help" by Erica Campbell. I cried out to God, and at that moment, He wrapped His loving arms around me. At that moment, I knew that I was not alone. And although my earthly parents transitioned, He reminded me that He was with me and that He would be more of a father to me than I've ever experienced before. I continued to cry out to Him, as the river of my heart flowed.

Tears Make Up The Journey

The source of a river is usually found in high places, such as hills or mountains. A river can have more than one source. Some rivers begin where a natural spring releases water from underground. Regardless of where, every river has an initial source, a place where it begins its journey. And like streams, your tears flow from a source— but it's the ending point, we may never know! Our tears make up an essential part of our journey.

All tears are not bad. The Word of God gives us a clear perspective:

- "Those who sow in tears shall reap with shouts of joy!" (Psalm 126:5)

- "For his anger is but for a moment, and his favor is for a lifetime. Weeping may tarry for the night, but joy comes with the morning." (Psalm 30:5)

- "Serving the Lord with all humility and with tears and with trials that happened to me." (Acts 20:19)

- "The eyes of the Lord are toward the righteous and his ears toward their cry." (Psalm 34:15)

- "The righteous cry and the Lord heareth, and delivereth them out of all their troubles." (Psalm 34:17)

- "A time to weep and a time to laugh, a time to mourn, and a time to dance." (Ecclesiastes 3:4)

- "He will wipe every tear from their eyes. There will be no more death or mourning or crying or pain, for the old order of things has passed away." (Revelation 21:4)

- "Put my tears in Your bottle." (Psalm 56:8)

No matter the source of the tears you've cried throughout your life, find comfort in knowing that they were prayers to the Lord. And although you may not have uttered any audible words, know that God is in tune with your heart, and feels the weight of your tears.

It's Okay To Cry

Sometimes people look at tears as a sign of weakness. But in actuality, it can symbolize the total opposite! It's a natural reflex that occurs when you're happy or sad. And as a result, you may experience great relief.

When I was in my early twenties, a friend of mine cried all the time. I made fun of her because I hardly ever cried. I didn't understand why I didn't cry until I embraced the development of my relationship with God.

As a result of our connection, my emotions surfaced. The walls of my heart were broken. My vulnerability was exposed, as I felt safe opening up to God. And throughout that process, God expanded my capacity to be more compassionate and more connected to the feelings of others. I was better equipped to help others, as I understood how to embrace my emotional side.

Sometimes, it's easier for women to be more emotional than men. Some men view it as a sign of weakness and may say that women are far too emotional. And in response to such a claim, I can speak on behalf of several women by expressing my view that it is very becoming for a man to be man enough to show his emotional side.

"When Jesus saw her weeping, and the Jews who had come along with her also weeping, he was deeply moved in spirit and troubled... Jesus wept."

— JOHN 11:33, 35

If Jesus wept, why can't we? As the Savior of the world, He holds power to redeem us back to our Father God in heaven. But despite His incredible strength, He wasn't ashamed to cry. Oftentimes, when we are afraid to cry, it may be a result of pride. There may be several factors that prohibit people from releasing what should naturally occur. Some tears are controllable, and some aren't. But despite our awareness, they may flow without our intention.

Tears will never stop because they are a part of life. *Are you crying tears of sadness or tears of joy?* Most times, your tears are affected by your season. But no matter what could be taking place, we should never allow our sad tears to flourish. Though your tears may have started out in sadness, they will end with joy, after experiencing God's love and healing, while you further your journey to wholeness. Your perspective will affect your outcome.

Deal With It

After you've accepted the situation, it's time to deal with it. Sometimes, that can be the biggest task! If you don't, you run the risk of experiencing that vicious cycle of pain. You could be repeatedly confronted with a situation that brings back memories of that deep pain. *Do you want to keep putting yourself through that?* Some people die with this pain. But that isn't what God wants for us! And although pain is a natural part of life, healing is still available.

Throughout the process, accept that it's best to have support.

> "Carry each other's burdens, and in this way, you will fulfill the law of Christ."
>
> — GALATIANS 6:2

You can't do this alone. Scripture says, "It's not good for man to be alone." But even if you aren't married, everyone can benefit from this truth. We have to understand that we help each other grow and get through different seasons in our lives.

> "A generous person will prosper; whoever refreshes others will be refreshed."
>
> — PROVERBS 11:25

It's important for us to be there for one another. A simple conversation can lead to an impartation of godly counsel. Receiving this can bring you to life, where you walk away feeling like you can conquer the world. Through much prayer and feeding on the Word of God, this posture can be maintained. The Bible is our sword, our secret weapon against all the things that we deal with in this life. There's a fight on the inside and the outside — may the strong man win.

"No man can enter into a strong man's house, and spoil his goods, except he will first bind the strong man; and then he will spoil his house."

— MARK 3:27-29

REFLECT/ JOURNAL

RESOURCES FOR CHAPTER THIRTEEN

Refer to the 30 Day Devotional
Day 20: "Promised Potential"
(*Available November 2021*)

To help with planning,
scan below to purchase the
Visionary's Planner.

13

HAVE FAITH IN YOUR FUTURE

Many are in high expectation for specific things to come to pass! However, knowing the end of a thing may be good, but also difficult— especially when the present doesn't resemble anything close to your expected future! And once you receive what you expected, it may be a great feeling of relief! However, there's always going to be something in life to work through. It just may be something different.

IF ONLY...

At times, we may think that as soon as we achieve something, life would be better! Youngsters may fantasize about being an adult so they can do things their way and not answer to anyone. Teens may desire to have a job so that they can get their own place. Singles may wish that they could meet the right person in order to be happy. Dating couples may rush into a marriage, thinking that all of their dreams would suddenly come true. Prospective leaders may think that when they finally start their business or ministry, things would be easy. Prospective parents may think that having children and starting a family would make things better for them. Individuals with stressful lives may wish that they can travel more in order to have peace of mind. And almost everyone can relate to the following thought, "If I can just save money and make six figures, I'll be set!" *If only...if only!* These are all desires that address the outward need, but none will address what's going on inside; these are just exterior fixes.

Likewise, I fell prey to that mentality, as well. At the age of 20, I wanted to buy a house. And if I pursued that path, knowing what I know now, I probably wouldn't have considered it. At the time, I didn't have enough confidence in the process. My credit wasn't high enough, and I didn't feel like I made enough money to support my desire. So, I continued along the journey of renting for several years, thinking that if I only had a house, that life would be so much better for me.

Without the peace of God, nothing will be better. We must learn to trust in God and be content with the state that our lives are in. We cannot be carried away by our current reality that we lose sight of the fact that there is a future approaching. Trust in God. Be patient. He knows exactly what He's doing!

Upon trusting God, I saw the manifestation of my faith. About twenty years later, I was finally at a place where I was ready to buy a house. Around that same time, I met my husband, who had already purchased a house in his twenties. What I desired to do, my husband already established. He bought a house, not realizing that we would meet twenty years later, which allowed me to have the house that I always wanted.

This shows us the supreme benefit of trusting in God. No matter how life seems, anything apart from His influence cannot make your life better. In order to receive the promises of God, we must demonstrate the faith to receive.

MAINTAIN YOUR POSTURE OF FAITH

Even if your future hasn't arrived yet, continue to have faith in what's to come. While watching others, it may be hard to maintain focus. It may seem as if everyone else has a picture-perfect life, leaving you behind in the dust. But remember that no matter what you have and who you know, your life will never be picture-perfect. Of course, that would make life so much easier, but it's not reality.

The lesson of life is to learn to make the best out of what you've experienced and use it to push you into a greater experience! We can't stop writing the story because someone scribbled on our paper. Erase it or tear it out, but keep on writing, and one day, someone will benefit from your persistence to keep going! *What is more rewarding— quitting or persevering?* To know that God has given you an assignment and that you have completed a portion of it is so rewarding. So continue to set goals and develop your plans. Nothing compares to the fulfillment of your purpose. Have faith that it will come to pass!

"But without faith, it is impossible to please him; for he that cometh to God must believe that he is and that he is a rewarder of them that diligently seek him."

— HEBREWS 11:6

Because of God's excellence in all that He does, we can trust that He will fulfill every plan that He has established for us. All we have to do is our part, which is to trust that He will do what He purposed. Living a life of faith establishes consistency— a lifetime of seeking Him! And as we seek Him, He advises us on the next steps to take!

INTRINSIC FAITH

All of us have been wired with a natural mechanism on the inside to believe and have faith. A child that does not know he can walk may attempt to stand up after crawling and rolling over for months. He may think about it first, observe others doing it, and then study the atmosphere. He may know he has legs after seeing them move, but not in the same way others are utilizing theirs. But over time, it'll become easier for him to figure it all out. God gave us legs, as they are used for walking. Likewise, our minds are programmed to function the way they've been designed.

God gave us faith to believe, and we are expected to do just that! It pleases Him when we fulfill that divine purpose. Oftentimes, we believe, even before we know that it's something God put in us to do. *Do you realize how important faith is?* When you have faith, you have formed a level of trust with God. That can only come from a relationship with Him. To believe in something you aren't aware of takes bravery. Believing in the invisible in a faithless world, when everything dictates the opposite, takes divine assistance. It's not hard to believe in something that's right in front of your face! But it can be difficult to believe in something that doesn't appear to reflect what you heard from God! Regardless of what we see, we must know the power of faith— the power we possess!

Jesus said:

"Because you have so little faith. Truly I tell you, if you have faith like a grain of mustard seed, you can say to this mountain, 'Move from here to there,' and it will move. Nothing will be impossible for you."

— MATTHEW 17:20

This Scripture shows us that we can command a mountain to move from here to there. And because of what God has placed on the inside of us, the power of faith can activate manifestation.

REFLECT/ JOURNAL

RESOURCES FOR CHAPTER FOURTEEN

Refer to the 30 Day Devotional
Day 13: "Encourage Yourself"
(*Available November 2021*)

Scan below for the Prayer
of Salvation and Prayer of
Restoration

For Access
Use Password: Listen

14

ACCEPT YOUR NORMAL

What's *normal* to Believers may seem strange to others. Our normalcy may be different, and at times, also difficult to grasp. What we call normal may be weird to others. And what may seem normal to us, may label us as an outcast to some.

Growing up, I had to accept the fact that I was different and wasn't designed to fit in every environment I was in. Even before I gave my life to Christ, I didn't fit in. One of my cousins told me that there was something different about me when I was little. Even one of my friends from high school thought I was saved while we were in school together. To her surprise, I told her that I didn't receive Christ as my personal Savior until I was seventeen years old, which was after I graduated from high school.

Whether you know it or not, what you are destined to do will be evident in your life before you actually begin. What's on the inside of you will easily shine through because that's what you're made of. You will look like what you shall become, and you will start doing it before "it" becomes a "thing," because that's who you are and what God wanted you to be! He made it that way so that no one can take the credit. That was His doing. You will meet people in life that will help nurture your purpose and bring it out into the open. Regardless of your background, and no matter how tumultuous your past may have been, it all worked out to bring you to where you are today!

Throughout my life, I felt rejected, abandoned, and sometimes misunderstood. But to know that God understood and accepted every part of me into His family was all worth it. But as a result of feeling rejected, abandoned, and misunderstood, I was desperate to find true, unconditional love. I initially began to search for fulfillment in other people, not realizing that they couldn't give me what I desperately needed. There are always limitations with humans, as people cannot fully embody the fullness of God's love. But as Believers, we can allow God's love to flow through us to others if we've surrendered to Him. However, we must understand that there will always be restrictions because we are not God. That's why God wants us to fully rely on Him for what only He can give us. He promised that He would never leave us nor forsake us and that He would be there until the end of the world.

"The LORD himself goes before you and will be with you; He will never leave you nor forsake you. "Do not be afraid; do not be discouraged."

— DEUTERONOMY 31:8

"And even if we make our bed in hell, He is there— all because He loves us so much. If I ascend up into heaven, thou art there: if I make my bed in hell, behold, thou art there."

— PSALM 139:8

YOUR FIRST CHOICE

Most people have a lot of responsibilities. Between work, ministry, and family, they may have a lot on their plate! That's why some people may be with you for a certain period of time, but eventually, they may unintentionally slip away. As a result, you may experience times when you desperately want to talk to someone about your problems, but those you feel comfortable talking with may be busy. But more importantly, God isn't. He is never too busy to help us. We are His first choice. *But is God our first choice? Do we run to Him first when we need to talk? Or, do we go to others first?* With God, all of our information is safe. And His response to our need will always be sound impartation and wisdom that no man can give. He may instruct us to reach out to someone else for assistance or to remain silent on an issue and endure it without sharing it with others.

"The LORD will fight for you, and you have only to be silent."

— EXODUS 14:14

But in order to know that, we must first go to Him. He will lead us in the direction we should go. That's why God should be our first choice—always! He desires that we prioritize His presence in our lives by choosing Him first.

THIS IS HOW IT'S SUPPOSED TO BE

No matter how many flips and turns your life has made from birth up until this point, I want you to know that your life was designed just for you. We may sometimes say, "It's just too much!" or "Why do things have to be so difficult?" *But is it really?* Perhaps we haven't taken the time to evaluate how we see things. We must understand that God truly loves us and that He won't put any more on us than we can bear!

> "No temptation has overtaken you except such as is common to man; but God is faithful, who will not allow you to be tempted beyond what you are able, but with the temptation will also make the way of escape, that you may be able to bear it."
>
> — 1 CORINTHIANS 10:13

And if you have ever questioned God's judgment about a matter, just know that He is perfect in all of His ways!

> "As for God, His way is perfect; the word of the LORD is proven; He is a shield to all who trust in Him."
>
> — PSALMS 18:30

Have you ever cried out in agony: *"God if You are in control, why didn't my life turn out better than this?"* This question is common to those who've experienced a life of pain— the negative consequences of sin. And as a result of the fall of man— from purity into sin— we've inherited the consequences of sinful patterns and behaviors. However, the Blood of Jesus became our saving grace! When we acknowledge that sin has consumed us, Jesus responds to our faith and cleanses us from all unrighteousness. When we believe and receive Jesus Christ as our personal Lord and Savior, we are accepted into the Family of God. But despite being in a sinful world, and affected by the repercussions of sin, we are not held captive to its consequences! We are being preserved until the Day of Judgement, when we will enter into the New Jerusalem— a new heaven and a new earth! But despite knowing this, we may still experience moments where we question God's ability to do what He promised us because of how things look. Instead, we should refocus that question on ourselves.

FINDING NORMAL

Are we holding up our end of the bargain? Have we done what we agreed to do? In those moments, we should remember that God will always do what He said He would do! We should also re-examine God's Word to us. *Did He promise us a picture-perfect life?* No. *Did He say that everything would go as we planned?* Not at all! But regardless of what we may face in life, God's grace will enable us to come out of our situation stronger, wiser, and more equipped to help others! And as a result of our breakthrough, we should have a better attitude and a greater appreciation of God's goodness — always ready to share our testimony with others! What's the purpose of having good news if you keep it to yourself? We should be agents of grace who share God's wisdom, giving hope to others in need!

"For we must all appear before the judgment seat of Christ, so that each of us may receive what is due us for the things done while in the body, whether good or bad."

— 2 CORINTHIANS 5:10

But just before my breakthrough, I had a moment with God. He asked me, *"What if this is the way your life was supposed to be?"* Hearing this brought me to silence, as the tears dried on my face. I will never forget this day. I was in my dining room— walking, crying, and praying! God gave me the answer that I needed. I understood *my normal* from a new perspective.

Trying to explain what normal looks like may be challenging. Normalcy isn't something you can put in a category or describe based on situations that occur. However, expressing my normal may help you to understand yours.

Change was my normal. And if I'm completely honest, I had trouble accepting when negative changes happened and when circumstances didn't go as planned. But in those times, God stepped in and made a miracle out of what I thought was a mess.

> "And shall not God avenge his own elect, which cries day and night unto him, though He bears long with them? I tell you that he will avenge them speedily."
>
> — LUKE 18:7-8

And when it was over, I realized that I was made to handle whatever came in my direction. In those moments, I realized how strong I was with God's help! And so much creativity was birthed out of a season of pain.

TRANSITION & BIRTH

In 2011, my dad transitioned to be with the Lord. It was a pivotal point in my life. I didn't know how to respond to what took place. We had a very close relationship; I was daddy's little girl. Being the youngest of two older brothers, I am the little girl that my parents prayed for. My mom and dad always wanted a girl, and God gave them what they wanted. My dad named me Crystal, and my mom gave me my middle name, Cerise. My dad told me that if he ever had a little girl, he wanted her name to be Crystal. I was loved and adored by my dad, and I soaked up every bit of it.

After my dad's transition, Holistic Ministries was birthed. Despite the pain, something beautiful came forth. So I learned not to dismiss the pain, as sometimes pain is good.

Pain is an indication that there is a problem. And sometimes, if you never experience pain, you will never know that there is an underlying issue on the inside. For example, some people may experience pain in their bodies. And because they may not know how serious it is, the pain may sometimes be ignored for a while, before realizing that it's time to go to the doctor's office to determine the root of the pain. And once the physical examination is finished, the doctor may discover an illness. And whether or not the illness is terminal or temporary, the pain is what prompted the inquiry to take place. So, sometimes, painful situations may bring things to the surface that we need to deal with.

However, on the other side of the pain, there is healing, birth, and creativity.

After my pain: God healed me, birthed vision through me, and sparked an influx of creativity within me! The very things that caused me pain were the very things that needed to be addressed. I depended on my dad for many things, which is common for most young girls— especially daddy's girls. I not only relied on him for physical protection, but also for spiritual protection. He was so insightful and full of wisdom. He walked in great obedience to the Lord. I learned so much from his walk with God, and I questioned him about everything concerning my growth in the Christian faith. My dad was a great prophet of God. He was very knowledgeable about the mysteries of God. Sometimes, I sat around him just to pick his brain about things that I did not understand. Our conversations were always very enlightening. So, when my father transitioned, I asked the Lord, "What am I going to do now when I need help with questions that I don't understand? And, when I need an interpretation of my dream?" The Lord replied, "I was here all the time; you can ask me!" So, it was during this time that I developed a closer relationship with God, as I couldn't rely on my dad to give me the answers that God could give me Himself. I grew to a place of maturity in a lot of areas, as I no longer depended on my dad.

Sometimes, you don't realize just how dependent you are on others, even as an adult. It was a good feeling to know that he had my back. Whether it be physical, spiritual, or emotional, my dad was my strong support. Therefore, it was an interesting journey, getting to know God as my support, as well as embracing different sources of wisdom through other people that God used. I grew to understand that sometimes people are close to us for a specific season. Furthermore, God sends people in our lives to impart specific things at specific times. And sometimes, when those seasons are over, those relationships may grow apart. This is something that many have struggled with. When people leave our lives, we may see it as rejection or abandonment, when in actuality, it simply means that the season has ended. God may have intended for the relationship to last until a specific goal or purpose was accomplished. And afterward, it's time to move on. On the other hand, there are some people that will be in your life indefinitely. They may be the ones who are always close to you. Then, there are others who may be close to you for a season, but become distant after that season is up. And if we aren't careful, both parties may blame each other for how the dynamics of the relationship shifted, when in actuality, it may have been God who allowed it to happen that way. It takes maturity to walk away from a relationship when it's necessary, even when there's nothing wrong. And throughout it all, we must remember that through pain, there is a purpose. And even though it doesn't feel good— as it wasn't meant to *feel* good— it is profitable that we go through certain things in our lives to accomplish certain goals. *But are we open to these life-changing situations and transitions that may change the course of our entire lives?* That's why it's good to know what season it is in your life.

When you can properly gauge the season that you're in, it becomes easier to identify the *what* and the *why*. It's a dangerous place when you walk through life blindly, not knowing where to go or what to do! You may find yourself moving all over the place, doing everything but the right thing during a particular time. But when you submit to God's leading, He will guide you to where you need to be. And even if you are led to a new environment— where people think, move, and respond differently — when it's a God-ordained space, you will continue to experience peace wherever you are. That is why we must learn to trust God to lead our lives. He is aware of everything we need to be properly equipped for our destination.

PURPOSE REVEALED

As a young child, I wanted to do so much. So many things had my attention. Everything about fashion design, photography, modeling, and hair-styling truly interested me! And as I got older, I realized how my life incorporated all of those interests over time. I was able to see why I had such strong interests, even as a child; it was God's way of showing me the areas that He desired for me to work in.

Right after high school, I developed a passion for computers and administration. So, I attended school to develop those interests. Several years later, I decided to go to seminary school to learn more about the

Bible. While in seminary school, I was introduced to the idea of counseling. As part of my curriculum, I was required to take a counseling course. And from there, I furthered my interest and became a counselor. Following this, I was led to become certified in holistic nutrition. Little did I know that my certifications would contribute towards the foundation of Holistic Ministries, as this ministry deals with the whole person—spiritual, physical, emotional, and social. God was showing me that purpose is revealed in stages, but rarely all at once, as it would be quite overwhelming to grasp. Therefore, we must take our time through each stage.

It's important that we pace ourselves through life. Nothing can be rushed, as we must be prepared to handle what's next. Our minds have to be programmed, and our spirits have to be fortified for every phase of our lives. In grade school, you are taught information that's relevant to the level you're on. But before you are able to advance, you must be able to demonstrate your ability to properly apply the information you've been given. Oftentimes, this assessment is done through tests. And just like school, life is full of lessons and tests! *What have you learned from your last season? And have you applied it to your present phase of life?*

With every lesson, there is a problem to solve. Your life is the resolve to an earthly problem. *What have you been put here to solve and change?* Jesus had a mission. He came here to die and to save us from the penalty of sin.

"For the wages of sin is death, but the gift of God is eternal life in Christ Jesus our Lord."

— ROMANS 6:23

JESUS IS THE EXAMPLE

Jesus saved the world and left a legacy behind after His three years of ministry. He gave us the blueprint for how to live life and how to operate in ministry.

> "Verily, verily, I say unto you, He that believeth on me, the works that I do shall he do also; and greater works than these shall he do; because I go unto my Father."
>
> — JOHN 14:12

He demonstrated love to everyone He met and healed many He came in contact with. He showed his followers that there wasn't a ritual for the miraculous, as He performed no miracle the same. He demonstrated that we must follow the leading of the Holy Spirit. His wisdom extends far beyond the wisdom of man! Man is limited in his ability to understand.

When presented with an issue, doctors may go through a process of elimination. It's customary for doctors to go through a standard system of question and answer in order to determine the presenting problem. They may initially ask general questions, but then ask more specific questions, in order to identify what's going on under the surface. Then, through a process of elimination, they may be able to determine the problem. And as a result, they may prescribe medication to cure the ailment they believe is present. However, doctors are limited in what they know and can do. But by the grace of God, many are able to utilize their God-given abilities to create machines and advanced technology to bring healing to those that are sick.

RECEIVE BY FAITH

In the Bible, there was a woman with an issue of blood, who needed divine intervention. Her condition was beyond what any doctor could fix. And despite her financial situation, she was unable to buy the healing she desperately needed. Her story reveals the truth about the power of faith.

> "And there was a woman who had had a discharge of blood for twelve years, and who had suffered much under many physicians, and had

spent all that she had, and was no better but rather grew worse. She had heard the reports about Jesus and came up behind him in the crowd and touched his garment. For she said, 'If I touch even his garments, I will be made well.' And immediately the flow of blood dried up, and she felt in her body that she was healed of her disease. And Jesus, perceiving in himself that power had gone out from him, immediately turned about in the crowd and said, 'Who touched my garments?' And his disciples said to him, 'You see the crowd pressing around you, and yet you say, "Who touched me?"' And he looked around to see who had done it. But the woman, knowing what had happened to her, came in fear and trembling and fell down before him and told him the whole truth. And he said to her, 'Daughter, your faith has made you well; go in peace and be healed of your disease.'"

— MARK 5:25-34

When you read this passage of Scripture, there is so much that can be gathered. This woman truly reverenced Jesus and His power. She knew that if she just touched Him that she would be healed. She heard the reports of His past healings and miracles from those that He came in contact with. And from this example, we, too, can learn to receive all that we need from God by faith. God has a reputation for stepping in on time and doing a complete job. If we stay on the potter's wheel, He will continue to mold us and shape our character. This woman heard about Him and pursued Him, knowing that she would be healed.

"'Can I not do with you, Israel, as this potter does?' declares the Lord. 'Like clay in the hand of the potter, so are you in my hand.'"

— JEREMIAH 18:6

COMMUNE THROUGH YOUR SENSES

Consider how God made us. We were given the distinct abilities to see, hear, smell, taste, and touch. And through each of our five senses, we were designed to commune with Him.

- **Eyes (Vision)**

    Although God has blessed us with eyes to see in the natural, He wants to understand how to see the things that have taken place in the spirit. For some people, seeing is believing. And God has no problem with proving Himself to us.

    Elijah and the Prophets of Baal

    "Then Elijah said to them, 'I am the only one of the Lord's prophets left, but Baal has four hundred and fifty prophets. Get two bulls for us. Let Baal's prophets choose one for themselves and let them cut it into pieces and put it on the wood but not set fire to it. I will prepare the other bull and put it on the wood but not set fire to it. Then you call on the name of your god, and I will call on the name of the Lord. The god who answers by fire—he is God.' But there was no response, no one answered, no one paid attention... Then Elijah said to all the people, 'Come here to me.' They came to him, and he repaired the altar of the Lord, which had been torn down."

    — I KINGS 18:22-24, 26, 30

    The showdown between the false prophets of Baal and our True and Living God was an unforgettable display of true power. This moment caused many to erect the altars of their heart because the physical altar they built in honor of a false god did not respond.

God stepped in and performed a creative miracle so that no one could get the credit, but Him.

Have you ever seen this happen in your life? You may have wavered in your faith and wanted to stay neutral due to your lack of confidence in God. You may have wanted to play it safe by not choosing a side.

- "Elijah went before the people and said, 'How long will you waver between two opinions? If the Lord is God, follow him; but if Baal is God, follow him.'" — 1 Kings 18:21

Some Israelites worshipped God and Baal when it was convenient for them. They worshipped God to please the prophets and worshipped Baal to please Jezebel, in order to receive favor from her.

- "Their heart is divided; now they are held guilty. He will break down their altars; He will ruin their sacred pillars." — Hosea 10:2

Do you have a Baal in your life? Who or what is it? Anything that we give more attention to or put in place of God serves as a Baal in our lives. So, *do you totally rely on God and give all the glory back to Him? Or, do you credit others, even though they may just be His vessels?*

- "Has a nation ever changed its gods? (Yet they are not gods at all.) But my people have exchanged their glorious God for worthless idols." — Jeremiah 2:11

- "The Zidonians lived among the people of Canaan. They were idolaters who worshipped other gods. "And if it seems evil unto you to serve the LORD, choose you this day whom ye will serve; whether the gods which your fathers served..." —Joshua 24:15

But when God showed forth His supreme power, this was an opportunity for those that worshipped idols to turn from their wicked ways and acknowledge the True and Living God. And at that moment, that was an opportunity to choose to be on the Lord's side.

- "Let them, therefore, give us two bullocks; and let them choose one bullock for themselves, and cut it in pieces, and lay it on wood, and put no fire under; and I will dress the other bullock, and lay it on wood, and put no fire under." — I Kings 18:23

The two bullocks symbolized two opinions. The bullock that was cut represented our own self-will and sacrifice. This is the sacrifice that we make for things that will not benefit our spiritual growth. But if we sacrificed our will for God's will, our lives and the lives of others will prosper. The bullock that was not cut represented an open heart before God, giving Him our best. The worshipper with two opinions gave a broken sacrifice because part of them was divided in heart, mind, and spirit. Elijah made up his mind whose side he was on. And his offering reflected his life of sacrifice to bring glory to God. So, when he adorned the other bullock, he wanted to give God his best. What we present to God must be our best. God looks upon the posture of our heart. So while the people were making their sacrifice to please people, Elijah prepared his sacrifice to please God.

This fascinating occurrence was a symbolic act that took place at Mt. Carmel. It demonstrated how God was working behind the scenes to establish something deeper than proving that their gods had no power. His intention was to show just how much God loves everyone by allowing us the choice to choose and serve Him for the rest of our days.

God's Covenant With Abraham

"But Abram said, 'Sovereign LORD, how can I know that I will gain possession of it?' So the Lord said to him, 'Bring me a heifer, a goat and a ram, each three years old, along with a dove and a young pigeon.' Abram brought all these to him, cut them in two and arranged the halves opposite each other; the birds, however, he did not cut in half. Then birds of prey came down on the carcasses, but Abram drove them away. As the sun was setting, Abram fell into a deep sleep, and thick and dreadful darkness came over him. Then the Lord said to him, 'Know for certain that for four hundred years your descendants will be strangers in a country not their own and that they will be enslaved and mistreated there. But I will punish the nation they serve as slaves, and afterward, they will come out with great possessions. You, however, will go to your ancestors in peace and be buried at a good old age. In the fourth generation, your descendants will come back here, for the sin of the Amorites has not yet reached its full measure.' When the sun had set, and darkness had fallen, a smoking firepot with a blazing torch appeared and passed between the pieces. On that day the Lord made a covenant with Abram and said, 'To your descendants, I give this land, from the river of Egypt to the great river, the Euphrates— the land of the Kenites, Kenizzites, Kadmonites, Hittites, Perizzites, Rephaites, Amorites, Canaanites, Girgashites, and Jebusites.'"

— GENESIS 15:8-21

In Genesis 12, God inaugurated an unconditional covenant with Abraham. But three chapters later, in Genesis 15, Abraham requested a visible sign to verify God's promise to him. And God did just that. He confirmed His Word to Abraham by establishing a covenant with him. And although the natural descendants of Abraham proved to be unfaithful in the years to come, God never went back on His covenant with Abraham. Instead, it set the stage for the New Covenant to be revealed through Christ's Blood.

God will forever stand true on His Word. But to receive the promises of God with a pure heart, we must sacrifice the desires of our flesh. A covenant with no sacrifice is just words. But when we are willing to tear up the agreement with hell and reaffirm our agreement with Heaven, then God will consume everything that's not like Him and receive us.

After reading both passages of Scripture that pertain to Elijah and Abraham, one notable similarity stands out. In both instances, God performed covenant-confirming ceremonies. In each instance, it involved the sacrifice of an animal and its blood to establish a covenant.

In Jeremiah 34:18-20, we can understand God's heart towards breaking covenants.

"'The men who have violated My covenant and have not fulfilled the terms of the covenant they made before Me, I will treat like the calf they cut in two and then walked between its pieces. The leaders of Judah and Jerusalem, the court officials, the priests and all the people of the land who walked between the pieces of the calf, I will hand over to their enemies who seek their lives. Their dead bodies will become food for the birds of the air and the beasts of the earth.'"

— JEREMIAH 34:18-20

Here, we see that passing between the parts of a slain animal was a customary practice for establishing a covenant. And if a covenant is broken, we can see just how significant it is to God. Symbolically, the action of walking between two parts of a slain animal indicated that both parties agreed to the consequences of death if a covenant was broken. They agreed to be slaughtered like the sacrificial animal that was used in the covenant ceremony. And this is the same ceremony that took place when God established His covenant with Abraham.

When we reflect on what took place at Mt. Carmel, we can see God's faithfulness through the covenant He established with Elijah, which stemmed from the original Abrahamic covenant. God, Himself, consumed Elijah's sacrifice, displaying that He is the judge of sin and that He will purge us of our impurities. God showed the false prophets that He is the only one that can judge and purify. And unless God consumes us, He won't have free rein to flow in our lives. We won't be able to establish a covenant with Him unless we are broken before Him. When we are broken before Him and separated from the contamination of the world, our sacrifices are like a sweet aroma before Him.

- "I beseech you therefore, brethren, by the mercies of God, that you present your bodies a living sacrifice, holy, acceptable to God, which is your reasonable service." — Romans 12:1

- **Ears (Hearing)**

God has blessed us with the natural ability to hear. But although we can hear naturally, He desires that we utilize our spiritual ears to hear, also!

"Now when they heard this they were cut to the heart, and said to Peter and the rest of the apostles, 'Brothers, what shall we do?' And Peter said to them, 'Repent and be baptized every one of you in the name of Jesus Christ for the forgiveness of your sins, and you will receive the gift of the Holy Spirit. For the promise is for you and your children and for all who are far off, everyone whom the Lord our God calls to himself.' And with many other words, he bore witness and continued to exhort them, saying, 'Save yourselves from this crooked generation.' So those who received his word were baptized, and there were added that day about three thousand souls."

— ACTS 2:37-40

After Jesus ascended back to the Father, He gave us access to the precious gift of the Holy Spirit. God demonstrated His power after Peter preached a message to the people about the Holy Spirit. Not only did the people who just heard about Jesus need to witness the manifestation of the Holy Spirit, but the Apostles that walked with Jesus needed to experience it, also. The Holy Spirit's visitation took place in the open so that those who heard the Word of God would believe and repent.

Acts 2 demonstrates that God has already gone before us and has laid out the red carpet. *But are we giving the proper presentation of the Good News? Are we witnessing in our sphere of influence and demonstrating the manifestation of the Word of God in our lives to those we come in contact with?* If not, we haven't spoken up loud enough! Don't be afraid of rejection, as some will reject the Gospel, but some will not. People are waiting for a message of hope to be released. And sharing the Good News will fulfill every need that they didn't know how to articulate. Upon receiving salvation, there is a pull to experience deeper levels of intimacy with Him. And after we've been beckoned to come closer to God, it is our responsibility to respond through action.

- "But be ye doers of the word, and not hearers only, deceiving yourselves." — James 1:22

- **Nose (Smell)**

    Fragrant, aromatic substances, including: ointments, anointing oils, and incense, are mentioned several times throughout the Bible. Many times, they were used for spiritual, medical, or personal purposes. When a useful substance, such as olive oil, didn't smell particularly good by itself, adding a fragrance added pleasure, a sense of significance, and a distinctive association.

    Several fragrant spices and oils are mentioned in the Scriptures. The sweet incense burned on the altar in the tabernacle was made of equal parts of stacte, onycha, galbanum, and pure frankincense. This was for this sacred use only; God did not permit any personal use, as He stated, "Whoever makes any like it, to smell it, he shall be cut off from his people." The Scriptures indicate that the burning of incense is a type of prayer going up to God. Our prayers are a sweet smell to God.

    The word "perfume" occurs only three times in the Old Testament. Proverbs 27:9 is commonly referenced for its use of the word.

    "Perfume and incense bring joy to the heart, and the pleasantness of a friend springs from their heartfelt advice."

    — PROVERBS 27:9

    The word "ointment" occurs fifty-eight times in the Old Testament. It is usually translated as "anointing oil." In other places, it is translated as "incense" or "sweet incense," which means a fragrant incense.

    The predominant oil referenced in the Bible is olive oil. Olive trees grow naturally in the Middle East. The word "oil" is derived from the word "olive." It has many purposes, and is commonly used in food, cosmetics, and medicine. It is an essential substance that's included in many rituals, incorporated in funerals, and used for fuel in lamps.

In the United States, the popularity of olive oil is increasing, as people rediscover its health benefits. Olive oil has been commonly used for wounds, bruises, and putrefying sores. It is viewed as an emollient to soothe and soften the skin. Olive oil is also used to anoint the sick, as it was a symbol of the Holy Spirit that God used to miraculously heal. And it wasn't a coincidence that God chose to use this oil as a symbol of healing, as it has a host of great health benefits.

- **Mouth (Taste)**

In the Bible, God references our ability to taste His goodness. In doing so, His intent isn't for us to use our natural mouths, but to use our spiritual taste buds in order to experience or perceive His goodness.

- "Taste and see that the LORD is good; blessed is the one who takes refuge in him." — Psalm 34:8

- "How sweet are thy words unto my taste!" — Psalm 119:103

- "That by the grace of God, he should taste of death for every man." — Hebrews 2:9

- "For as touching those who were once enlightened and tasted of the heavenly gift, and were made partakers of the Holy Spirit, and tasted the good word of God, and the powers of the age to come." — Hebrews 6:4-5

- **Hands (Touch)**

    The ability to touch is referenced frequently through the Word of God. In most cases, touching directly correlates with healing, as those who were touched by God were made whole.

    - "And besought him that they might only touch the hem of his garment: and as many as touched were made perfectly whole." — John 14:36

    When I received my healing, it wasn't to prove to anyone that I had changed. Christ died for me, and I wanted to walk in the freedom of new life. It was exhausting to live life in bondage to something that was killing my dream and hindering my progress. I desired to be free so that I could complete my assignments and testify to others about the goodness of God. I wanted others to be able to receive the same freedom I experienced.

BE AUTHENTIC

We can't fit God's plans into an idealized version of life that we desire. We must accept the reality of how things are. But in an age where hardly anything is real and authentic, it may be hard to see things for what they really are.

Most of what we consume in America isn't real. And almost everything authentic has a matching faux version that's trying to take its place. But regardless of its attempts, inauthenticity cannot compare to authenticity, as it cannot provide the full benefits that come with being genuine. A knockoff version cannot produce what the original version was designed to do.

In the Body of Christ, this same conflict takes place. There are many who pretend to be what they feel people want. They desire to be what they perceive is expected of them. However, this creates a dilemma, as real results cannot be produced from an inauthentic version of you. This dilemma is the reason why we may not see the full manifestation of what

God intended in our lives, in our churches, and in the Body of Christ at large. We may have fake friends, form fake relationships, and fake church! When authenticity is missing, we suffer. We may produce what we think people will accept to appease their comfort levels, but it will never work out that way. Only God's way will promote change. And in order to do it His way, we must operate the way He created us to be— our authentic selves. When we are real, people will be drawn to Him, not our churches, conferences, and events. We won't have to backflips and summersaults to attract people by appeasing their flesh. God, in His infinite wisdom, had a purpose for everything he created. And we honor Him as Lord when we operate in our authenticity.

THE INSIDE WAR

In order to be authentic, you must know the truth. But because there's a constant battle between truth and lies, it it's hard to know what to believe. A part of you may want to believe in the truth, while another part of you may find comfort in the lies. So, in order to properly discern and cling to what's true, we need the guidance of the Holy Spirit. And even when our spirit man is awakened to the truth, our flesh may seek to fight against it. But through the power of the Holy Spirit, we are able to conquer the opposition of the flesh.

> "For the flesh desires what is contrary to the Spirit, and the Spirit, what is contrary to the flesh. They are in conflict with each other, so that you are not to do whatever you want."
>
> — GALATIANS 5:17

When we read the Word of God, our spiritual eyes are continuously opened to the truth. Communing with the Holy Spirit is like having private lessons with God. And when He teaches us new things, the application of it in our lives demonstrates our understanding. We can then share our wealth of wisdom by teaching others. The understanding we receive from God, we should share! The Bible is the manual; the Holy Spirit is the instructor. Without the spiritual illumination of the Holy Spirit, it's just words without demonstration. It's like giving a textbook to a student and expecting the material to be fully understood. God understands that we need teachers to help us understand and apply the truth we've been given. Likewise, the teaching element in the church is needed. Preaching breaks the chains of bondage, sets you free, and opens your spiritual eyes. Once you are free, it's much easier to receive what you're taught because you are no longer bound.

STAY CONNECTED

Consider what it's like to be captured. The first thing kidnappers do is tie your hands and feet so that you won't move or be able to run away. They may even tape your mouth shut so that you can stay silent and not cry for help. When you're bound, you may not see any real progress, as you can't move or speak. You may be in a condition where you're too weak to help yourself. This is similar to what the enemy does, as his goal is to limit your growth.

Many times, the enemy's first tactic is to isolate you and keep you stagnant. At that moment, your mind may tell you that you're okay, but without anyone else around to challenge you, you may not really know the true condition you're in. You may not be able to track your progress without seeing healthy examples of it around you. Similarly, children learn how to walk and talk by seeing others do it. As humans, we learn from others. And the power of connection cannot be underestimated.

Both good and bad influences can come from those around you. And even if your intent isn't to engage, the atmosphere may seek to conform you to its standard. So, if you're around creative and productive people, you may eventually become like-minded. If you're around lazy and unmotivated people, you may find yourself lacking the drive to move forward. That's why people who lack drive may find it uncomfortable to be around motivated people who are always progressing. Oftentimes, you may find that jealousy can easily set in within the relationship. However, we must realize that we are all students with the same teacher, learning at different paces, on different levels, and with different capacities to receive.

Despite our differences, the Holy Spirit is not limited to our varied capacities. If we are teaching, we can teach for hours, under the power of the Holy Spirit. When we are open to His direction, the knowledge and wisdom of God can flow like a river through us. And as He flows, we both are being washed by the cleansing power of His Word. God's Word will flush out the junk, making room for His presence. And as the teacher, we will be open to receiving more divine revelation while teaching. Therefore, both the giver and the receiver will benefit from this divine cleansing.

GET CLEANED

When waste stays in the body too long, it can make you sick. Over time, it can cause bacteria to spread in your body, and you may eventually become septic. Sepsis is a widespread infection, causing organ failure, and dangerously low blood pressure. This is a life-threatening condition caused by a severe localized, or system-wide infection. Emergency treatment may include: supplemental oxygen, intravenous fluids, antibiotics, and other medications. This treatment can kill everything alive in you. That's why God is so particular about cleansing— both naturally and physically!

Why do you think God desires to give us a new heart? That's because what's in your heart can contaminate everything else that's healthy and functioning normally. And although sepsis is a natural illness, the same condition can take place in the spirit realm. In the natural realm, once your heart stops beating, oxygen will no longer travel efficiently throughout the rest of your body, regardless of how healthy your organs are. And eventually, those organs will die due to the lack of oxygen in your body. Blood and oxygen work together to sustain life. When God breathed into the nostrils of man, he became a living soul. His breath gave us what we needed to survive. And now, when we breathe, we continue to take in oxygen that is carried throughout our bloodstream and distributed throughout our bodies. And the blood is so significant. *Life is in the blood.*

"For the life of the flesh is in the blood: and I have given it to you upon the altar to make an atonement for your souls: for it is the blood that maketh an atonement for the soul."

— LEVITICUS 17:11

NEW LIFE BY THE BLOOD OF JESUS

The blood of Jesus is needed to wash away our sins. At birth, we were born into a life of sinful contamination. And everything we accumulated throughout life pushed us closer to spiritual death. However, the Blood of Jesus altered our destiny! Through His Blood, we have a new life with Christ and have been born again. The old man has died, and a new man was resurrected. We received a spiritual blood transfusion and became new in Christ— *new* blood and *new* life!

Receiving salvation is the most life-changing decision we can ever make. When you hear the Good News of Jesus Christ, it prompts a change in mindset, which stimulates a response. And when you respond by accepting Christ into your heart, you will have new life. But although you received new life, it requires your mind to be constantly renewed so that you don't slip into unhealthy thinking. Your mind must be renewed regularly.

"Do not conform to the pattern of this world but be transformed by the renewing of your mind. Then you will be able to test and approve what God's will is—his good, pleasing, and perfect will."

— ROMANS 12:2

When you are born again, you will receive a new life, a new heart, and a new path. But you will still have a memory! You may still have the mindset that controlled your old way of thinking— the mindset that preceded your new life. Sin has brainwashed you. Your purpose was compromised by a sinful nature that happened after your conception. But even though this sounds like a set up for failure, God changed the ending to the story!

Everything around us in this world dictates failure. It's not until divine intervention takes place, that we are saved from its damnable fate. When we are saved, we receive eternal life and all of the promises of God. He will preserve us and bring us into a lifestyle full of peace. We have the Almighty God backing us up and fighting for us! And for as long as we are on this earth, up until we transition into eternity with Him, He will forever be our peace.

God's love for us is a beautiful story of rescue and redemption. He finds us, rescues us, and redeems us back to the Father. In Him, we have the hope of eternal glory.

Prayer of Salvation

My Beloved Father, I acknowledge that I need your help in this life on earth and that I cannot do anything without You. I realize that You had a resolution for the fall of mankind that started with Adam, but I thank You that the story didn't stop there! So, today, I acknowledge that I have sinned, and I ask You to forgive me of them all. I believe that You sent Your son Jesus Christ to die as a sinless sacrifice so that I can be free from sin and have a relationship with You. I receive my free gift of eternal life today. And I receive Your perseverance and guidance through the person of the Holy Spirit, to guide me through the rest of this life.

In the Name of Jesus, Amen.

Prayer of Restoration

My Beloved Father, I thank You today for Your grace and mercy that has covered me, even in the midst of my inconsistency, as it pertains to my relationship with You. I thank You for being faithful, no matter what, and reassuring me that there was nothing I could do to earn your faithfulness and your love. Forgive me for allowing life's circumstances and distractions from different areas of my life to separate me from You. Today, I rededicate my life to you— my mind, my heart, and my soul— I give you total control over me. Anoint me again. I thank You for never leaving me, and for being patient with me until I was ready to come back to you! Today, I choose to begin again!

In the Name of Jesus, Amen.

REFLECT/ JOURNAL

RESOURCES FOR CHAPTER FIFTEEN

Refer to the 30 Day Devotional
Day 30: "Charged & Ready"
(*Available November 2021*)

Scan below to listen to the
Finish Strong Declaration

For Access
Use Password: Listen

You were prepared to start fresh, and you are excited about the end. You can see the finalized product, but you don't quite know if you will keep the same tenacity and focus throughout the process. You have to be determined and persistent in order to follow through to the finish line.

15

FINISH STRONG

I started many things in my life, but I don't know why I faced so much difficulty completing them. So, I prayed and asked the Lord to help me to not just be a starter, but to be a finisher— and not just any kind of finisher, but a *strong* finisher! I wanted to finish everything I set out to do with excellence. In the past, there were several things I started out doing that took me much longer than expected. However, I was determined to finish and received my High School diploma, cosmetology license, Holistic Nutrition certification, and pastoral counseling degree from seminary school. But before then, things weren't always easy, as I went through a rebellious stage prior to getting myself back on the right track towards accomplishing my goals.

FINISHING HIGH SCHOOL

During my senior year in high school, months before I was ready to graduate, I decided that I was going to drop out of high school. I was in a rebellious state and did everything opposite of what I was supposed to do. I was not concerned with staying on the right path. This was due to the company I surrounded myself with. Later, I realized that bad company could negatively influence you unless you're strong enough to maintain your position and lead them. However, it's healthy to stay around people that are further along than you, so that they can help you along your journey, as you both move in the same direction.

It's ironic that the person I spent time with was also a high school dropout. I was in a dating relationship with him and was getting ready to head down the same path. But my dad prayed and released the love of my Heavenly Father that surrounded me. After running away from home, I was beckoned by my father to come back. When I disappeared, I later learned how many were concerned for my wellbeing. Even my school administration announced my name and that I was missing over the intercom, in an attempt to get help from those who might know how to find me.

Months later, I came back home. Like the prodigal son, who did not have to leave the safety and security of his father's home, I made an unwise decision to leave. I was lured away by my desire to experience the world, seeking to obtain something more valuable than what I already had. I later realized that it was time to go home, once everything I placed my confidence in for survival was gone— my money, so-called friends, and credibility.

The Prodigal Son

"The Parable of the Prodigal Son (also known as the parable of the Two Brothers, Lost Son, Loving Father, or of the Forgiving Father) is one of the parables of Jesus in the Bible, appearing in Luke 15:11–32. Jesus shares the parable with his disciples, the Pharisees, and others.

In the story, a father has two sons. The younger son asks for inheritance from his father, who grants his son's request. This son, however, is prodigal (i.e., wasteful and extravagant), thus squandering his fortune and eventually becoming destitute. As a consequence, he now must return home empty-handed and intend to beg his father to accept him back as a servant. To the son's surprise, he is not scorned by his father but is welcomed back with a celebration and a welcoming party. Envious, the older son refuses to participate in the festivities. The father tells the older son: "you are ever with me, and all that I have is yours, but thy younger brother was lost, and now he is found."

Just like the prodigal son's father, my dad welcomed me back with loving arms. Being back home, I was able to accomplish one of my major goals. I finished school, walked across the stage, and received my High School Diploma.

FINISHING COLLEGE & VOCATIONAL CERTIFICATIONS

Over time, I obtained my cosmetology certification, Holistic Nutrition certification, and seminary degree in pastoral counseling. It definitely wasn't easy, as many things took place that slowed down my progress. But I persevered and finished strong!

Taking the cosmetology test wasn't easy, but I was determined to obtain my certification. It took me six times to pass my cosmetology test. Demonstrating the practical application was easy, but understanding the theory portion was a challenge. However, even after five failed attempts, I kept trying and didn't give up until I passed. On the sixth try, I prayed and fasted for God to show me the parts I didn't know, and help me pass the test. He answered my prayer, and I was able to finish strong!

Obtaining my seminary degree took some time, as I stopped after my dad's transition. At the time, I completed two years of seminary school and struggled to finish due to the weight of everything that I experienced. However, God spoke through my Director, who encouraged me to keep going. He allowed me extra time to finish, and also offered a financial package to assist with the cost of seminary. I knew that God was telling me to continue, so I picked up the pieces and kept moving forward. In the end, I finished strong, and I am grateful to be able to use my pastoral counseling degree to help others overcome challenging times.

Most recently, I obtained my Holistic Nutrition certification. I began the process of certification throughout the period of my engagement, but stopped to focus on planning my wedding. During my first year of marriage, I regained my focus and continued along the process. I failed the test twice, but felt led to reach back out to my teacher before taking it a third time. I asked her to compare both tests and compute my overall score based on the answers that were answered correctly. When she examined both tests, she noticed that one answer was different— it was answered correctly on one test. Therefore, she was able to factor in points for that question, which gave me the passing score that I needed to obtain my certification. Having this certification allowed me to continue pushing forward so that I could fulfill the vision God gave me through Holistic Ministries and finish strong!

Obtaining my college degree and certifications, along with many other classes and workshops helped to upbuild, nurture, and activate the gifts within me. That's why it's important for us to remain teachable, as life is full of lessons. Growth doesn't stop just because we've arrived at one destination. Learning isn't a destination, it's a continual path. After we've mastered one thing, God releases another teachable experience around the corner.

"Give instruction to a wise man, and he will be still wiser; teach a righteous man, and he will increase in learning."

— PROVERBS 9:9

FINISHING MY LIFE STORY

Fifteen years ago, I began writing my life story. However, I didn't finish it until 2020. I decided to come in agreement, co-laboring with my Father in Heaven. I made a covenant with Him, agreeing that I would complete everything that He put me here to do on this earth. In the words of Dr. Myles Monroe, "we should all die empty," having fulfilled the vision God placed within us.

So, where are you in the process? Have you taken steps to advance your *vision? What have you been sitting on for years?* Seize the moment! God wants us to tap into the creativity that He has invested in us. There are many doors that haven't been opened! We already have access, but we need to open the door. Just take the first step, and God will reveal His truth while bringing clarity to our lives!

The year of 2020 is the year of clarity! You may not understand how it all fits together. Understanding why things happened in your life that have led up to this point may not make sense. However, we must accept that our process, our challenges, and even our victories are part of *our normal*. And God uses every facet our normal to birth His vision!

It's time to advance your vision! What's your purpose, business, ministry, invention, or idea? Many aren't aware of their purpose in life. This isn't a bad place to be in, especially if you are still seeking it out. God wants us to tap into the creativity that He has invested in us. There's a door that has yet to be unlocked in us all. There are many doors that have yet to be opened. In a vision, I saw a haze covering some doors. Over time, the haze cleared up so that the doors could be seen. Once it was gone, I saw the keys to the doors. They were hanging in the air and accessible. This vision confirmed that we have access. All things are made new! God is revealing and bringing clarity of vision in our lives! Things will be so clear in the seasons to come. Stay connected to God and develop a relationship with Him. To know God is to know yourself, as we were created in His likeness and image. The one and only way to know who we truly are is to go to the Originator, the person who made us— God our Father!

"For in him, we live and move and exist. As some of your own poets have said, 'We are his offspring.'"

— ACTS 17:28

FINISH YOUR STORY

Over 2,000 years ago, the Bible was written. According to the Guinness World Records, as of 1995, the Bible is the best-selling book of all time, with an estimated five billion copies sold and distributed. The Bible is the inspired Word of God given to man. It not only shows us how the world came into existence, but gives us divine revelation from Biblical principles, regarding how to live a life of freedom in Christ that God intended. It also transcribes the lives of many who have made mistakes, overcome struggles, followed God's instruction, and sometimes disobeyed.

Today, many of us have stories of victory and inspiration. And many times, God has given us divine wisdom and revelation for the current era that we're living in. Therefore, we have to keep writing our literary pieces, droplets from heaven that are inspired by God, so that others can be encouraged to push beyond what was, what's presently happening, and continue to evolve into who God called them to be!

Furthermore, both the Bible and our life stories can be considered anthologies. An anthology is described as a published collection of writings. Oftentimes, when you look in the Bible, you will see various books written by different authors who have contributed to its formation. Regarding our life stories, whether or not we decide to compile them in one book or write them individually, others can walk away with a glimpse of hope for their future because of our bravery to be transparent about our lives.

The Lord said to me, and perhaps others, as well, "Crystal— your past, your story, and your testimony mark the end of the last chapter of your life. You have overcome, and healing has taken place. You are made whole. Old things have passed away, and all things are made new! Today marks the beginning of your new chapter. Your story isn't over. Your new one begins today!"

So take action **today**. Step out on faith. Trust God with the process. He's kept you thus far, and He will not leave you now! So, embrace your normal! Say *yes* to your purpose! And finish your story!

REFLECT/ JOURNAL

AFTERWORD

Crystal Love's book titled *Finding Normal* is more than a personal memoir. It's a story of her growing up in Baltimore (she spent a few years as a teenager in North Carolina), the major challenges she faced as a child and young adult, and how her Christian faith helped her find her life's calling as a therapist, a lay church leader, a mother, an entrepreneur, and a devoted spouse.

She shares her story of personal struggles and how her deep faith sustained her and enabled her to use this experience in her vocation as a practicing therapist. And she goes on to talk practically about the need to understand oneself better. And very importantly, she concentrates on understanding the love of Jesus as reflected in the Christian and Hebrew Scriptures. It can give us the strength to fight distractions, pulling us away from our true calling.

Crystal's many experiences are supported by scriptural passages and stories of the loving support of her family and friends who were there for her when she needed them.

AFTERWORD

What struck me the most about Crystal's story and her counsel to readers is its relevance to today's world. Her message reminded me of one of the most profound themes in the work of Gabriel Moran, my advisor and mentor during my graduate studies in religious education at Manhattan College and Union Theological Seminary. In two of his books -- *The Theology of Revelation* and *God Still Speaks: The Basis of Christian Education*, Dr. Moran explains many Christians believe in God's revelation through the Hebrew and Christian scriptures as static. They believe that God's intervention in lives ended in the first century. This is not true. Yes, the scriptures are sacred, but God continues to reveal Himself in many different ways today.

Crystal understands this phenomenon as she explains, "When we are in a relationship with Him, God can help us find answers to the questions we have in our hearts. Through the Word of God, prayer, and others in the body of Christ, we can receive those answers and attain resolve for every question and concern."

As a monk or member of a lay Catholic religious order – the Brothers of the Christian Schools – I lived a monastic lifestyle during my early years as a brother. We kept silent virtually all day long. As a reminder that every person is a child of God, when we needed to speak, we would break our silence by saying to another brother, "Live Jesus in our hearts," and respond, "Forever." This was an affirmation of what some theologians refer to as the mystical body of Christ. We are all God's children, and Crystal, in her book, expresses this clearly and inspirationally.

God continues to inspire, and His presence is real. It remains in our present lives. How? Through the experiences and events that continue to touch those lives.

Robert Coles, one of the greatest 20th century writers – a child psychiatrist whom I've met and corresponded with – won a Pulitzer Prize in literature for his book series, *Children of Crisis: A Study of Courage and Fear in the South*. One of his books was about Ruby Bridges, a six-year-old black child in the 1950s who was the first black child in an all-white school in New Orleans. In a talk I heard Coles give about children who were the first to enter white schools and the hatred they encountered, he commented on their experience and the presence of grace or the presence of God in their lives. This was a leading factor in their growing up successfully.

I believe grace plays a significant role in Crystal's life. It has showered her with the resilience and love of Christ that has enabled her to succeed in becoming who she is today. It has also enabled her to share what she learned in the practical steps she includes in recognizing God's presence and turning one's life around.

"Finding Normal" is an inspiring work that reflects God's presence in our lives and gives us solid guidance on how to show God's love through those in our families and our communities.

Sean Gresh
Author, Becoming a Father (Bantam Books)
Adjunct Professor, Northeastern University,
College of Professional Studies

ACKNOWLEDGMENTS

The completion of this book would not be possible without the love and support of many throughout my life. All of my experiences have shaped me into the woman I am today, forming the foundation for Finding Normal to be birthed.

∾

I would like to extend a special dedication to my parents, the late Jacob and Exemea Schroeder:

I thank you both for getting married and praying for the little girl you always wanted! I guess after two boys in a row, you were ready to experience a girl. And here I am, 40 years later, writing about you in my first book! I knew you would be proud of what God has done and will continue to do in my life. While this book has excerpts from my life, it would take a lifetime to pull out the great and precious moments you both afforded me to have as a child, into my teenage years and adulthood. Learning about God and what Christ Jesus did for us on the Cross was the most expensive gift you could have ever given me that money couldn't buy! I don't know where my life would be if you two weren't my parents, as you both set my foundation in place.

Before you both transitioned, I expressed my gratitude to you. But no matter how much I try, I cannot express my appreciation enough! From birthdays to holidays, to teaching me how to ride a bike and cook, mom and dad, you both get a standing ovation! Prophet Jacob Schroeder and Missionary Exemea Schroeder, thank you for showing me what true love is all about. I took significant lessons from every part of your lives.

∽

Dad, you taught me how to keep pushing through adversity and never put down the plow when it's time to work! You worked so hard in the natural and the spirit. You stood on what you knew God spoke to you. It amazed me how devoted you were to God, and how God used you prophetically to bless and warn people about what He revealed to you as it pertained to the past, present, and future. You had such a deep love for God's people and a servant's heart. I watched you sacrifice so much for the sake of spreading the Gospel of Jesus Christ. You were not ashamed to share your love of God with everyone, no matter where you went! I am so glad to have witnessed your sacrifice and your strength in my personal life, as my father and mentor. I remember watching you host revivals, heal the sick, raise the dead, and renew sight to the blind. I was so amazed to see you— someone I was around every day— do something so powerful, right before my very own eyes! You were a man of great faith. And in admiration of your walk with God, I wanted to walk in that same level of faith.

∽

Mom, what a loving mom you were! I remember coming home some days with my room cleaned and dinner fixed. Oh my— I absolutely loved your cooking! Mom, you would have been a great chef, as one of your dreams was to start a catering business called Dee's Catering. I know it would have been successful because all of your food was delicious and seasoned to perfection! You left such an imprint on my heart of bravery and determination.

As the daughter of the late Pastor Dr. Lillie Mae Bryant, you had a strong spiritual background, which contributed to the way you raised me to love God with my whole heart. I loved hearing the story of how you met my dad in church. You both were young and saved while serving the Lord. What a match made in heaven!

I remember watching you teach Sunday school, something you were so passionate about! You were so good with children, and they all loved you. One day, you stood in front of the church after Sunday school, asking the class questions as a review. I didn't say much, as I was always too shy to answer. But all of the other kids participated in your lesson. Not to mention, they also knew that you had a bag of treats!

Mom, you had a boldness in you that screamed to come out. I was so glad when you answered the call to become a missionary. And although you only got a chance to preach one sermon, three months before you passed away, you shared the love of God to many people throughout your day-to-day journey.

When you first became ill, I remember going into your room and seeing many Scriptures on your wall. Your faith in God touched me. One of the Scriptures that moved me was Psalm 118:17.

"I shall not die, but live and declare the works of the Lord."

— PSALM 118:17

I love how this Scripture became an essential part of your testimony, as you testified of God's power to bring you back to life after your heart stopped beating during surgery! Your love for preaching the Gospel of

Jesus Christ was so contagious. When I found a book of your sermons, I knew that I needed to share portions of them with everyone. And although it was emotional, Tony and I touched on some of your messages, as together, we preached your eulogy. That was a moment in time that I will never forget. God gave us both the strength to be brave and honor your legacy by sharing your love for Him through your messages.

～

Mom and Dad, although you are no longer here with us, God has truly blessed us with the great support of family throughout the years. But from time to time, I still reflect on our family dynamic, and how fun it was growing up in your house. I never really realized how much you sacrificed until I got older.

Growing up with brothers, Eric and Antonio, was so exciting. Having siblings meant automatic playmates, but they were also my protectors! And although I grew up with boys, I still had my girly side. I remember when one of my kindergarten teachers told you both that I was a good student, but always played with boys? I'm sure that made you laugh, as you had to explain to my teacher that I had two older brothers, which made it easier for me to adapt to playing with boys over girls. Hearing you tell this story was so funny to me, as I'm sure my teacher did not expect that explanation. But those were the fun times, back when life was simple!

Saturdays mornings— I can never forget! You both made sure I had something to eat. As a little girl, I had to get up early so that I could eat first to ensure that my hungry brothers didn't eat all of our breakfast. And although I barely ate as much as they ate, I still wanted something!

As a child, I didn't realize how good I had it, and the sacrifices you both made for me. You both made sure that I had wonderful opportunities in life. I didn't fully understand the depth of your sacrifices until I heard stories about your love for me. This was true love defined. My brothers and I had everything we needed because of you both, and I can look back and say that I am so grateful for all you have done for us.

~

I thank God for my brothers, Eric and Antonio Schroeder:

Eric, you are the artist who is very creative in drawing and writing poems. You are a lover of the Word of God and an extreme worshiper! I remember how much fun it was playing Bible trivia during the holidays. You and dad were not allowed to play because it wasn't a fair game, as you both knew all of the answers. We called you both "The Bible Scholars!" You always made sure that I was focused on my dreams and moving forward in life. That's what big brothers do!

Tony, you are the artist, graphic designer, photographer, father, husband, prophet, mentor, and entrepreneur. You are full of creative ideas and vision! You are also "My Twin." Together, we are "The Dynamic Duo." Because of how connected we are and how much everyone says we look alike, we really could have been twins. We have tag-teamed many sermons together and are always able to connect both in the natural and spiritual.

Brothers, you both are remarkable. You are the best brothers that a little sister could ever have. In all actuality, you know I'm the big sister, even though when I say this, you both laugh!

~

I thank God for my grandmother, the late Pastor Dr. Lillie Mae Bryant:

Grandma— oh, how I remember those Sundays when I wanted to stay over your house after morning service to go back to evening service with you! I remember you being so gentle and sweet to me. You are one of the most loving, generous, sweet, gentle, powerful, and anointed people anyone could ever be in the company of!

As a little girl, I remember seeing you preach and shout on the pulpit at church. Oh, how the entire church would get excited and stirred up by your moving messages of deliverance. I remember when I would get sick as a little girl, and my parents would just bring me straight to your house, and being with you would make it all better. You were the first person that I thought of when I was getting ready to preach my first sermon. I was in the office and looked out to see everyone there, and nervousness and anxiety set in. At that moment, I thought to myself, if only my grandma was here! But the mere thought of you brought peace, and my anxiety dissipated.

I always felt such peace being with you, grandma. I will forever cherish the memories of you in my heart for the rest of my life.

~

I am so grateful for my beloved husband, Terry William Love, Jr.:

Babe, you are a man of great faith, wisdom, and integrity. As you have served as an authority in the Baltimore Police Department for twenty years, God has given you that same stance in the spirit realm— to cover and protect your family, loved ones, and those that come across your path. Throughout this journey, God has protected you every step of the way. He has given you the grace to do so in the natural and spiritual realm. Your last name served you well, as it is the true definition of who God is. I am grateful to share the same name.

In 2013, God allowed us to cross each other's path. Meeting you that day was unexpected. I saw a man of prayer and vision standing before me in a meeting. I was blown away by your physique, but what truly grabbed my attention was your posture of authority in prayer. I saw a man of God, walking in his God-given purpose. It was love at first sight for me.

Months before we met, I asked the Lord to send me my husband from heaven, wrapped in a bow. I wanted someone like my dad! This was an earnest request, as I wanted him to be sent directly from my Father in heaven. And that's exactly what He did! He gave me you! All I wanted was a partner who I could share a friendship and walk into destiny with. Our foundation was a friendship that blossomed to a beautiful love story that only God could have put together. You have been crucial in helping me make important decisions, enlightening me to see it from another perspective! God used us both to aid in each other's spiritual growth and heal our hearts from past wounds. I call it surgery of the hearts! Years later, we allowed God to seal the deal, and our souls became one— a threefold cord that cannot be broken.

ABOUT THE AUTHOR

Crystal Love, a native of Baltimore, Maryland, is a wife, mother, servant, and prophet in the Body of Christ. She is a certified Christian counselor, licensed cosmetologist, and certified Holistic Nutritionist who walks boldly in her purpose. She utilizes her academic background and experience to assist and push others to *find* out their purpose, *focus* on it, and *accomplish* it! Under the umbrella of her organization, Vision Advancement, she helps her clients navigate the process from start to finish.

In 2012, God gave her a vision entitled Holistic Ministries. This ministry was birthed out of a season of pain. During this time, she grieved her father's death, while trying to establish herself as a single mother. At that stage in her life, she recognized the correlation between her overall wellness and spiritual health.

These three Scriptures had a significant impact on Crystal:

- "When Jesus saw him lying there and learned that he had been in this condition for a long time, he asked him, "Do you want to get well?" — *John 5:6*
- "Beloved, I wish above all things that thou mayest prosper and be in health, even as thy soul prospereth." — *3 John 2:2*
- "The thief cometh not, but for to steal, and to kill, and to destroy: I am come that they might have life and that they might have it more abundantly." — *John 10:10*

Upon meditating on these Scriptures, the depth of God's love was revealed to her. She recognized the impact of one's total wellness, as a grounded life glorifies God! From that moment forward, she approached wellness from a holistic standpoint, understanding the significance of balance, consistency, and discipline within every aspect of a person's life.

And to this day, Crystal Love is dedicated to serving people abroad. She has a deep, heartfelt passion for seeing others become healed and delivered spiritually, emotionally, socially, and physically.

Beloved, I pray that in all aspects, you may prosper and be in good health, just as your soul prospers.

— 3 JOHN 1:2

For more books and updates:
www.crystallove-theauthor.com